KEEP THE
SIBLINGS
LOSE THE RIVALRY

Also by Todd Cartmell

The Parent Survival Guide

10 STEPS TO TURN YOUR
KIDS INTO TEAMMATES

KEEP THE
SIBLINGS
LOSE THE RIVALRY

DR. TODD CARTMELL

GRAND RAPIDS, MICHIGAN 49530 USA

Keep the Siblings, Lose the Rivalry
Copyright © 2003 by Todd Cartmell

Requests for information should be addressed to:

Zondervan, *Grand Rapids, Michigan 49530*

Library of Congress Cataloging-in-Publication Data

Cartmell, Todd, 1962–
    Keep the siblings, lose the rivalry : Ten steps to turn your kids into teammates /
Todd Cartmell.
        p. cm.
    ISBN 0-310-24680-6
    1. Interpersonal relations — Religious aspects — Christianity. 2. Sibling rivalry.
I. Title.
BV4597.52.C37   2003
248.8'45 — dc21   2002014245
                                                          CIP

Interior design by Nancy Wilson

Printed in the United States of America

---

03 04 05 06 07 08 09 /❖ DC/ 10 9 8 7 6 5 4 3 2 1

To Rodney,
I am proud to be your brother, and always will be.

CONTENTS

FAMILY TIME DISCUSSION GUIDES

ACKNOWLEDGMENTS

I'd like to express my gratitude to the team at Zondervan for their work on this book, with a special note of thanks to Sandra Vander Zicht for her helpful guidance and suggestions. I am also indebted to my family, for the time they allowed me at the computer and for being the greatest wife and kids anyone could ever hope to have.

I looked down into the saucer-sized brown eyes of my two-year-old son, who at that moment had just taken the incredible plunge into life as an older brother. Without his fully realizing it, his days as an only child were forever gone. As I sat in the overstuffed delivery-room chair and relinquished the video recorder duties to my father-in-law, I watched Jacob take his first look at the little reddish-purple face that emerged from the hospital blankets.

"Say hi to Luke," I said, fighting back the tears welling up behind my eyes.

"Can I touch him?" was his response.

"Sure, pal. Right here. Real gentle," I said, guiding his hand to softly stroke the side of Luke's face.

"Can I hold him now?" Jacob asked, as one touch was evidently not a satisfactory way of meeting his new brother.

"Sure you can," I said, as I moved Jacob to my lap and let him hold Luke in his arms, while I supported his arms from underneath.

These were our first few moments together as a new-sized family. We walked over to the bed where Lora was resting, placed Luke in her arms, and marveled together at the spectacular event we were experiencing.

"Is he my baby?" Jacob asked out of nowhere. Lora and I both instinctively smiled at the childlike innocence of his question.

"Yes, honey," Lora replied. "He belongs to all of us. Luke is part of our family now."

At some point, a nurse informed us that they needed to take Luke to the nursery area for a short time of observation. Obediently, I placed Luke in the infant cart and began to roll him toward the nursery.

"Can I push him?" came Jacob's familiar refrain.

"That would be great if you would help me," I answered.

One of our favorite photos from that day is the picture of Jacob looking up at me with excitement as he and I rolled Luke toward the nursery. Whenever we look at it, we immediately smile as we are reminded of the sibling bonding that began to happen that day. The bonding we hope will go on forever.

As they begin their family journey, most parents are filled with anticipation of a warm, loving family that plays together, has fun together, and walks hand-in-hand through life together. In their mind's eye, they see images of nurturing and loving relationships between parents and children, relationships that flourish and bloom like a beautiful field of daisies swaying in the wind on a warm summer day. Brothers and sisters, instinctively appreciative of the unique strengths and richness each brings to the family, respond to each other with courteous smiles, always thinking of the other person first.

"Chad, you can go first on the computer today."

"Tamika, would you like the last cupcake?"

"Maxwell, I know you don't feel like going outside to pick up dog poop today, so I'll do it for you."

Then it happens.

Reality crashes in.

Allison: "Mom, he's touching me!"

Steven: "I am not!" *(with a mischievous grin)*

Allison: "Yes, you are! Quit lying!"

Steven: "I'm not lying! Quit trying to get me in trouble!"

Mom: "Both of you, stop it right now!"

Allison: *(starting to cry)* "But, Mom, he's doing it on purpose!"

Steven: "You're such a cry-baby."

Noah: "Mom, will you tell her to turn her stupid music off. I'm trying to do my homework."

Mom: "Honey, it's not that loud."

Noah: "Yes, it is that loud. Well, if you won't tell her then I will. *(shouting)* Michelle, turn your stupid music off!"

Michelle: *(shouting from her bedroom)* "I'm not bothering you. Go to the basement if it's too loud."

WHERE DO SIBLING PROBLEMS COME FROM?

Noah: "I don't need to go to the basement. *You* go to the basement and quit torturing the rest of us with your hideous
music. I can't stand it!"

Michelle: "Just because you can't get your work done at school is no
reason to give me a hard time. Mom, make him leave me
alone."

Noah: "Oh, so you're calling me dumb? Well, at least I'm not so
ugly that no boy in school wants to be seen with me."

Helpful gestures, cooperative playing, and cheerful laughter are
replaced with hurtful words, angry glares, and cries of unfairness. The
authors of the *Baby Blues* comic strip, Rick Kirkman and Jerry Scott,
humorously captured the length that children will go to incriminate their
siblings when they pictured a mother calling out from the kitchen in
frustration, "Who spilled the juice in here?"

The young daughter, playing with her blocks on the living room floor,
looks up with startled wide eyes and answers, "Not me! It wasn't me!
No, sir! It was . . . uh . . . Hammie [her younger brother]! Yeah! That's
who! Hammie must have done it. Tsk! That kid is such a brat!"

The mother, with a quizzical look, replies, "Yeah . . . and he spilled
that juice at the very same time he was taking a nap all the way at the
other end of the house."

Not missing a beat and sticking with her story until the end, the
daughter retorts, "Woo! He's worse than I thought!"

Sometimes the good days far outnumber the bad, making the sibling
squabbles easier to put into perspective. At other times, the good days
seem few and far between, as name-calling and tattling rule the moment.
All of us have been able to relate to the exhausted mother of three unruly
youngsters who was asked whether she'd have children if she had to do
it all over again. "Sure," she replied, "but not the same ones."

Getting through a meal without an argument over who had to eat the
most peas can seem like a gift from heaven. Our best efforts to squelch sibling problems before they start are thwarted by our children's ever-
expanding repertoire of ways to get back at each other. We sometimes feel
like the mother of the six-year-old boy who came crying because his little
sister had pulled his hair.

"Don't be angry," the mother said, trying to smooth things over. "Your little sister doesn't realize that pulling hair hurts." A little while later, the mother heard more crying, and she went to see what had happened. This time the sister was screaming.

Her brother looked up and innocently proclaimed, "She knows now."

No matter what our lot, we have all had our moments when, in the midst of listening to the hundredth argument over who was using the TV first, we have leaned our heads back on the couch, stared up at the ceiling in frustration, and silently mouthed the million-dollar question: "Why can't my children just get along?"

In your heart, you know this couldn't be what God has planned for your family. It certainly isn't the status quo you want to have to endure for the next ten to fifteen years. But still the question remains: How can children, who are supposed to have the closest of relationships, find every possible reason to bicker and fight with each other? Why is it so unbelievably difficult for them to get along?

FACTORS THAT INFLUENCE SIBLING RELATIONSHIPS

A glance through the Bible quickly dispels the rumor that sibling problems are an invention of the twenty-first century. They have been with us from the very beginning. The first sibling pair, Cain and Abel, ended up with a rivalry so strong that it resulted in murder, something we all hope will not happen in our households anytime soon. Not too long after this, Jacob swindled his brother, Esau, out of his family birthright. Years later, Joseph's brothers sold him to passing merchants as a slave when they could no longer stomach his stories of how he envisioned them all bowing to him one day.

We don't have to rely on biblical narratives to be reminded that sibling problems have been around for a long time; our own family experiences are just as convincing. In my sibling workshops, I often ask how many parents experienced conflict with their siblings when they were young. Almost everyone raises their hands. Many even admit to having purposely done mean things to their brothers or sisters when they were younger, just to get them into trouble. If only their parents had known the truth!

There are several factors that affect the quality of sibling relationships. Some of the most common include your children's temperaments, their individual strengths and weaknesses, and your parenting style. Let's briefly look at each of these factors now.

Temperaments

A child's temperament refers to her inborn tendencies, or the way she is "wired." Some children tend to be shy and cautious, while others are robust and energetic. One child is naturally flexible and compliant, while another tends to argue and throw tantrums.

It is not difficult to see how these differences in temperament can contribute to sibling conflict. John is an easygoing ten-year-old boy. He loves baseball, earns good grades, and has lots of friends. His eight-year-old sister, Samantha, however, is cut from a temperamentally different cloth. Samantha came fully loaded with a short attention span and a quick temper. She is a C student who takes longer on her homework than John ever did. When things go wrong, she becomes easily irritated and can launch a tantrum at the drop of a hat.

It comes as no surprise that John and Samantha are capable of getting on each other's nerves. Samantha feels like she lives in John's shadow, never measuring up to the boy who can do no wrong. John, on the other hand, has a hard time understanding why so much time and attention are given to Samantha, when all she does is cause trouble.

Individual Strengths and Weaknesses

Just as siblings have different temperaments, they also have different areas of strength and weakness. These differences show up in many areas, including school performance, physical ability, artistic talent, and social skills.

Consider Zachary, who has struggled with reading and writing since first grade while his older brother, Alex, earns straight A's with little or no study. Or Cindy, who finds piano lessons as exhilarating as a trip to the dentist while her sister, Tara, exudes beautiful music from her violin with effortless motion. These children who find themselves being outperformed by their siblings are in danger of accumulating feelings of jealousy and resentment that will inevitably fan the flames of sibling conflict.

Your Parenting Style

Parents have a strong influence on the quality of sibling relationships. Without realizing it, some of us treat our children in very different ways depending on their birth order. Other times, we fall into negative communication styles or fail to set clear expectations for how family members are to treat each other. Letting the busyness of life get the best of us, we can also fail to spend regular quality time together as a family, and allow family relationships to slowly grow stale with the passage of time. Let's take a look at each of these parental factors and how they influence sibling relationships.

Differential Treatment

It has been said that no two children have the same set of parents. While a reasonable amount of differential treatment is to be expected, based on a child's age and behavior, if we're not careful we can treat our children so differently that it actually contributes to sibling conflict. For example, it is easy to fall into the trap of expecting too much of the oldest child, babying the youngest child, and losing the middle one in the shuffle. As a result, the oldest child feels excessive pressure to do everything right, the youngest gets accused of being the favorite, and the middle child resents getting the short end of the attention stick.

"Wyatt is a classic middle child," Martha told me about her ten-year-old son as we stood outside my office door one afternoon.

"What do you mean?" I asked.

"Oh, he just gets lost between his older brother and younger sister," she said in the same matter-of-fact tone she would have used to tell me about the weather forecast.

What Martha failed to realize was that she is partially responsible for her son's plight. When all is said and done, perhaps Wyatt *is* left out in his family.

Birth order effects are not the result of your child's innate temperament, but are the result of your child's *experience* as the older, middle, or youngest sibling in your family. Regardless of their birth order, each of your children needs to know that he or she is an important and valued part of your family. It is Martha's job to make sure Wyatt knows that he

FOR A LAUGH

Ways to Handle Parental Frustration

Good	Bad
Squeeze a stress ball.	Throw the stress ball at them.
Count to ten.	Let the air out of their bicycle tires.
Take five deep breaths.	Excuse yourself from an argument and immediately mix a martini.
Read a good book.	Purposely forget to put the drinks in their lunch boxes.
Whisper a short prayer.	Remind the kids that they have just taken five more years off your life expectancy.

is every bit as important to his family as his older brother and younger sister. The way you treat each of your children (whether they are your first or tenth!) will play a large role in determining how their birth order will impact their sibling relationships.

Negative Communication Styles

The way our children see us communicate has a big influence on how they will learn to solve their own disputes when we're not around. When we get angry at our children's behavior, it is easy to succumb to the temptation to use disrespectful tones and words, mistakenly thinking that this will solve the problem. Amazingly, we get upset when our children do the same things.

"I can't stand it when my kids scream at each other," Greg lamented to me during a parent session.

"Why don't we get together as a family to see if we can teach them how to talk respectfully?" I suggested.

"Let's do it," Greg and Teresa both enthusiastically agreed.

In our family sessions, however, things quickly played out differently than I had been led to anticipate. As we talked through family problems together, it was Greg who first began to raise his voice and refuse to listen to anyone else's point of view regarding the issues we were discussing. The children's frustration with not being listened to was obvious from the exasperated looks on their faces. As the session continued, I watched Teresa sit passively by, giving way to her husband's headstrong style. It wasn't long before the children began to fight back, one by one, determined to be heard, no matter what the cost. Following their father's lead, they too refused to listen to other views and expressed their opinions with increasingly disrespectful words. When it was all said and done, the family discussion had gone in exactly the direction the parents had led it. As they say, apples don't fall too far from the tree.

Lack of Clear Expectations

The lack of clear and explicit expectations for how family members should treat each other will almost always result in increased sibling conflict.

Sitting in my office one day, Shirley told me that her three children regularly call each other disrespectful names. "Oh, they do it all the time," she said with a casual laugh. "Isn't that what brothers and sisters are supposed to do?"

What bothered me most was not the fact that her children called each other names but that Shirley was not upset about this hurtful sibling behavior. She assumed that name-calling was just a natural part of sibling relationships and made no attempt to stop it. As a result, her children were learning some bad habits, and she got exactly what she expected.

Insufficient Family Time

When families fail to spend regularly scheduled family times together, or when the emotional family atmosphere becomes muddied by constant fighting and bickering, disrespectful sibling behavior can become the accepted status quo, rather than the exception to the rule. Your children simply fall into the habit of being annoyed with each other and don't have enough positive interactions to offset this negative momentum. As we will discuss in Step One, the amount of positive family bonding time you spend together with your children will have a direct impact on the quality of their relationships when you're not around.

All of these factors are present to different degrees in different families and need to be immediately addressed whenever they are present.

We will discuss each of them in detail at different points throughout this book. However, there are three fundamental reasons for sibling conflict that have influenced *every* sibling relationship ever since Cain and Abel tried on their first set of Pampers. Let's take a look at our list of the top three reasons for sibling problems (drumroll, please).

THE TOP THREE REASONS FOR SIBLING CONFLICT

Reason #3: You have more than one child.

Logically, it all begins here. You have sibling problems because you own a set of siblings. This is not a bad thing; in fact, it is one of God's most wonderful gifts to you. But as soon as number two is on the way, you have to get ready for a whole new set of parenting challenges. Teaching your children to share their toys. Deciding who gets the last chocolate pudding. Trying to figure out who hit whom first. In short, challenges that come only with siblings.

Reason #2: Your children live in the same house.

If you are reading this book, chances are that not only do you have more than one child but you also have them living in the same house. Some of you are even bold enough to have them sharing the same room! (What are you thinking?!)

Have you ever asked yourself why your children have friends? They have friends because they don't have to *live* with their friends. They see their friends at school, at soccer, at gymnastics, and then they all go to their own homes. In other words, childhood friends are together for all the fun, highly rewarding activities, and they spend very little time sharing the boring, tedious activities of life together. Waiting a turn to go to the bathroom, picking up toys they didn't play with, listening to music they don't like, sharing the TV, deciding who gets the larger bedroom—these highly annoying activities are saved for whom?

That's right.

Siblings.

The closer the proximity and the more mundane activities your children share, the more opportunities there are for them to be frustrated and irritated with each other. Take sharing a room, for instance. Sharing a room gives your children a chance to learn important lessons about sharing and negotiating and can help them develop a close bond as they fall asleep talking or playing quietly together each night. But with this proximity come many opportunities for conflict, even for the closest of siblings. If your children do not share a room, don't feel left out; there will be more than enough opportunities for conflict to arise for them as well. Which brings us to the number one reason for sibling problems:

Reason #1: Your children's living-together skills are still developing.

The number one reason that your children have sibling conflict is that their living-together skills are still in the process of developing. In case you haven't noticed, living together with other people is not always easy. It means sharing the good days and the bad, the play times and the cleanups, the good moods and the days where someone woke up on the wrong side of the bed.

Over time, we hopefully develop a reasonable set of living-together skills, which are habits and behaviors that make us a decent person to live with. Living-together skills include (but are not limited to) negotiating, sharing, respecting other's views, being flexible, expressing feelings respectfully, responding to day-to-day aggravation, taking turns, and solving problems. This may sound like a dream list of everything you wish your children were doing. That's exactly what it is, as these important skills help your children to handle the frustrations that are part and parcel of family life.

Ten-year-old Jillian came home after a hard day of school, feeling upset that she only got a C after trying her hardest on her spelling test. Needing to get her mind off of school as quickly as possible, she made a beeline straight for the TV, hoping to relax to the mindless entertainment of a few cartoons. However, when she arrived in the family room, she found her six-year-old sister already engrossed in a children's video that Jillian had seen a thousand times and was in no mood to see again.

Feelings of irritation welled up in her chest like a heat-seeking missile looking for a target. And the target was lying on the family room floor right in front of her.

Jillian: "I can't believe you're watching that! Why do you always have to watch a stupid movie right when I want to watch cartoons?"

Rachel: "It's not stupid."

Jillian: "You've seen it a thousand times. Can't we watch something else?"

Rachel: "No, I'm watching this."

Jillian: *(getting frustrated)* "You always have to have it your way. You are so selfish."

Rachel: "I am not. Mom!"

Jillian: "I don't want to watch that stupid baby movie anyway."

Underdeveloped living-together skills in action.

In this case, Jillian needed to learn how to be flexible when things don't go exactly her way.

Being flexible when your grandiose plans for the universe have just been thwarted is one of the more difficult living-together skills to master, especially when you are not even old enough to drive. Jillian believed she should be able to watch TV whenever she wanted to (never mind that someone else was already watching) and that she had the right to treat her sister disrespectfully when things did not go her way.

Both of these unspoken assumptions are inaccurate. The TV does not belong to Jillian, and she has no guarantee that she will be able to watch cartoons anytime she wants to. Furthermore, it is not acceptable to treat another family member disrespectfully just because she had a hard day at school. A more appropriate set of assumptions would have been:

- The TV isn't always going to be available when I want it.
- I need to be respectful to Rachel even when I'm frustrated.

When confronted with the reality that she could not watch cartoons, Jillian could have made some different choices, rather than choosing to insult and aggravate her younger sister. This, however, would have required the use of another important living-together skill: problem solving. Jillian could have asked her sister when her movie would be done, found someone else to play with, or thought of something else that she could do (e.g., listen to music, play with a favorite toy, read a book). Any of these solutions would have worked better than starting a fight by insulting her sister's taste in videos. However, Jillian's underdeveloped living-together skills led her to respond to her sister in a disrespectful way.

The result?

Sibling conflict.

WHAT CAN WE DO?

Given these three fundamental reasons that cause sibling conflict in every sibling relationship, what are we to do? Let's examine our options.

We can't do much about Reason #3 (You have more than one child), nor do we want to. We enjoy having several children and we hold onto the hope that we can foster a positive family environment, siblings and all.

Reason #2 (Your children live in the same house) is equally out of reach, unless you want to consider sending all of your children to separate boarding schools in separate countries.

Nope. We must focus our efforts on Reason #1 (Your children's living-together skills are still developing). We must teach our children how to live together.

One of your primary tasks as parents is to help your children develop a finely tuned set of living-together skills. These skills will aid them in every facet of their lives, both now and as adults. And what better place to develop these skills than the family—an environment ripe with never-ending opportunities for teaching, growing, and learning.

In his Word, God has given us the guidelines we need to build healthy families and help our children develop their living-together skills. And in his wisdom, he has created your family to be the perfect classroom for doing just that.

And guess who got volunteered to be the teacher?

You.

So what can you do about those living-together skills?

A LESSON FROM THE GARDEN

Sometimes, the answers to our most difficult questions are no farther away than our own backyards. Regarding sibling relationships, we can learn a lot from the beautiful flowers growing just outside our windows. Bursting through the mulch-covered ground in various shades of breathtaking beauty, these flowers speak volumes about the process of growth.

In order to raise a healthy flower, there are three things you must do. You must:

1. Prepare the soil.
2. Plant the seed.
3. Provide the right environment.

In the same way that all three parts of this natural process are necessary for raising a healthy flower, they are equally essential for raising siblings who can live and grow together. Each part of this process is comprised of several steps that will build your children's living-together skills and can change their sibling relationships forever. The rest of this book is devoted to teaching you how to put these steps to work with your children. Here is a description of each part of the process and of the ten steps that can help your children grow strong, healthy sibling relationships.

Section One: Prepare the Soil

As any good gardener knows, you must take great care to prepare the soil before you plant your seed. Rich, fertile soil will produce a far healthier and more beautiful flower than will a dry lump of clay. With regard to sibling relationships, this means that your first step is to create the type of family soil that will produce the type of family bonding and relationships God desires.

To create a rich and fertile family soil, you will learn how to lead simple but powerful family bonding and teaching times with your children that will strengthen their sibling relationships. We will underscore the importance of appreciating the different traits and characteristics God has given each of your children and making a strong individual connection with each child. You will learn strategies for combating the divisive intruders of comparing, labeling, and competition and develop a plan for instilling your family soil with the important ingredient of respect.

Section Two: Plant the Seed

When your family soil has been tilled and an atmosphere of close relational bonding and respect has begun to be established, then you are ready to plant the seed. The "seed" represents the living-together skills your children must learn in order to develop healthy sibling relationships. There are three types of skills you can teach your children: communication skills, problem-solving skills, and sibling survival skills.

Each of these skills is essential for living together in harmony. In order for your children to work through problems together in an effective way, they must first learn how to communicate respectfully with each other. Then they must have a strategy for how to solve problems by coming up with solutions that work for everyone. Finally, there are five sibling survival skills that every sibling needs to know. They include responding to sibling aggravation, sharing, taking turns, showing flexibility, and forgiving each other.

For each type of skill, you will find ready-to-use plans for teaching and practicing these life-saving sibling skills with your children. As you help them improve their skills in each of these areas, you will find they will learn to solve more of their problems on their own.

Section Three: Provide the Right Environment

After enriching your family soil and planting the seed, you must then provide the right environment if your seed is to grow and blossom into the beautiful flower it was created to be. In terms of sibling relationships, this means that you need to provide an environment where your children learn some very important lessons. Here are the lessons you want them to learn:

- Treating each other respectfully pays off, and hurting each other does not.
- Taking the time and effort to communicate feelings and desires respectfully works out well, while screaming and name-calling do not.
- Solving problems the right way works out much better than fighting and bickering.
- They are always responsible for how they choose to handle a situation.

In other words, you want your children to learn that respectful sibling behavior pays off and disrespectful sibling behavior does not. Your family environment must nurture and reinforce your children's positive living-together skills and discourage their old, negative habits of treating each other disrespectfully.

The strategic and balanced use of positive reinforcement and negative consequences will create a climate in which your children can learn these important life lessons. After all, experience can be a good teacher, as long as it teaches the right things. You will learn how to use positive reinforcement and negative consequences to help your children experience the benefits of respectful sibling behavior and the negative outcome of disrespectful sibling behavior. You will also discover a creative team approach to help your children learn that working together is *much* more fun than working against each other.

HOW TO USE THIS BOOK

Each chapter of this book concludes with two sections designed to help you master the concepts and immediately apply them to your family. If you are reading this book as a married couple, use these sections to sharpen your grasp of the material and decide how you will apply them to your family as a parenting team. If you are a single parent, use these sections to think through the concepts and decide upon a strategy for applying them that fits you the best.

First, each chapter includes a set of "Questions for Reflection." This section consists of application questions that will help you think through the ideas in each chapter and customize them to your family situation. You will then find a "Practice Makes Perfect" section, which provides exercises for practicing the specific skills discussed in that chapter. Once you have worked through the Practice Makes Perfect exercises, you can find sample answers at the back of the book. Finally, to help you teach a variety of essential sibling skills to your children, you will find fifteen "Family Time Discussion Guides" at the end of the book. These are ready-to-use facilitator guides for fun and effective family-time discussions (with your kids!) that you can use to teach and practice the important skills discussed in each chapter.

Improving sibling interactions requires a two-pronged approach. First, as husband and wife, you need to be on the same page with each other so that you can approach sibling issues in a consistent and effective manner. If you are a single parent, you need to carefully consider how you will implement these approaches in a way that will realistically work into your schedule and can be consistently enforced. The Questions for Reflection and Practice Makes Perfect sections will help you to think through these important issues.

Second, you need to teach your children important family principles and living-together skills in a fun and effective way. This is where the Family Time Discussion Guides come in. Be creative and flexible with the ideas in the Family Time Discussion Guides, choosing the questions and activities that will work with your family the best. Use and reuse all or portions of these guides as often as necessary to reinforce these important lessons and help your children improve their living-together skills.

If you want to work through this material in a systematic way, either on your own or as part of a parenting or study group, here is an example of a twelve-week schedule that includes approximate times for reading and using all of the helpful tools.

Week 1

20 minutes: Introduction
20 minutes: Questions for Reflection

Week 2

20 minutes: STEP ONE: Create a Strong Family Bond
20 minutes: Questions for Reflection and Practice Makes Perfect
30 minutes: Family Time Discussion Guide #1: Our First Family Time

Week 3

20 minutes: STEP TWO: Connect with Each Child
20 minutes: Questions for Reflection and Practice Makes Perfect
30 minutes: Family Time Discussion Guide #2: You Are a Special Part of Our Family

Week 4

20 minutes: STEP THREE: Eliminate Comparing, Labeling, and Competition
20 minutes: Questions for Reflection and Practice Makes Perfect
30 minutes: Family Time Discussion Guide #3: God Has Big Plans for You

Week 5

20 minutes: STEP FOUR: Require Sibling Respect
20 minutes: Questions for Reflection and Practice Makes Perfect
30 minutes: Family Time Discussion Guide #4: The Family Respect Rule

Week 6

20 minutes: STEP FIVE: Improve Sibling Communication
20 minutes: Questions for Reflection and Practice Makes Perfect
30 minutes: Family Time Discussion Guide #5: Say It the Right Way, Right Away

Week 7

20 minutes: STEP SIX: Step toward Solutions
20 minutes: Questions for Reflection and Practice Makes Perfect
30 minutes: Family Time Discussion Guide #9: Let's Solve This Problem (for older children). For younger children, choose from one of the additional Family Time Discussion Guides for improving sibling communication (#6–8).

Week 8

20 minutes: STEP SEVEN: Teach Sibling Survival Skills
20 minutes: Questions for Reflection and Practice Makes Perfect
30 minutes: Family Time Discussion Guide #10: Responding to Sibling Aggravation

Week 9

20 minutes: STEP EIGHT: Reinforce Positive Sibling Behavior
20 minutes: Questions for Reflection and Practice Makes Perfect
30 minutes: Choose from remaining Family Time Discussion Guides on communication skills or sibling survival skills (#6–8 or #11–14).

Week 10

    20 minutes: STEP NINE: Use Sibling Consequences That Work

    20 minutes: Questions for Reflection and Practice Makes Perfect

    30 minutes: Choose from remaining Family Time Discussion Guides on communication skills or sibling survival skills (#6–8 or #11–14).

Week 11

    20 minutes: STEP TEN: Put Them on the Same Team

    20 minutes: Questions for Reflection and Practice Makes Perfect

    30 minutes: Choose from remaining Family Time Discussion Guides on communication skills or sibling survival skills (#6–8 or #11–14).

Week 12

    20 minutes: Conclusion

    20 minutes: Questions for Reflection

    30 minutes: Family Time Discussion Guide #15: Our Family Checkup

READY, SET, GROW!

Grab a snapshot of your family and look closely at it. You are looking at the family God has blessed you with, and your most substantial years of influence are already ticking away. Every ounce of energy you put into helping your children learn to follow God's guidelines for relationships will be worth it, both for the immediate benefits your family will experience and for the shaping influence that will forever be felt in the lives of your children.

The other day, our boys brought their Legos into the family room and were consumed in the challenge of building an elaborate maze of colorful walls, hiding places, and buildings for their little Lego men. I was working at a nearby desk and was able to see them out of the corner of my eye.

All of a sudden, Jacob looked up and blurted out a question. "Dad, if our Lego guys had to lose either their treasure or their family, which would be better?"

"What do you think?" I asked.

Jacob paused for a second, his brow furrowed in thought. "It would be better for them to lose their treasure, because then they'd still have their family," he replied, and then quickly turned back to his play.

"Buddy, I think you're right," I affirmed.

As I reflected on this curious exchange while writing this book, it occurred to me that this is what every parent of siblings wants to hear. You want your children to value their family relationships more than a TV show, a computer game, or the last cupcake. Whether they realize it or not, these relationships are one of the greatest lifelong treasures they will ever have. With that in mind, let's dive in and take a look at how you can prepare your family soil to produce the type of sibling relationships that you've always hoped you could grow.

QUESTIONS FOR REFLECTION

1. What are the hopes and dreams you have for the type of relationships your children will develop with each other?

2. What are some of the negative sibling behaviors that your children regularly exhibit that you would like to change?

3. How much do you think your children's temperaments, individual strengths and weaknesses, or your own parenting style (e.g., differential treatment, negative communication style, lack of clear expectations, lack of quality family time) affect their sibling relationships?

4. Make a list of five living-together skills that would improve the quality of your children's relationships.

5. Think about the three-part process for building healthy sibling relationships (e.g., prepare the soil, plant the seed, provide the right environment). Why do you think each part is important?

PRAYER SUGGESTIONS

Close this time with prayer, asking God to guide you as you embark on this new family journey. Pray that he will help your children be receptive to the new experiences they will have and the lessons they will learn. Reaffirm that you will be open to learning about your own strengths and weaknesses, trying new parenting approaches, and humbly letting God shape you into the parent he wants you to be.

PREPARE THE SOIL

CREATE A STRONG FAMILY BOND

Melanie was a fourteen-year-old girl whose relationship with her ten-year-old sister, Heidi, had been growing in parched, dry relational ground for several years. In a counseling session one day, I asked Melanie about her relationship with her sister.

"Do you and Heidi ever do anything fun?" I asked.

"Are you kidding?" Melanie retorted. "Why would I want to do anything with *her*?"

"Well, she is your sister," I replied, surprised by her distant response.

"We just annoy each other and we always end up fighting. It works out better if we just do our own thing," came Melanie's answer.

As Melanie spoke, I could almost tangibly feel the chill of this damaged sibling relationship. These two girls had hurt and annoyed each other until all the life had been drained out of their relationship. Luckily, there is hope for damaged sibling relationships like Melanie and Heidi's, and the first step is to create a strong family bond.

When family members have a strong family bond, it means that they feel valued by and connected with each other. It doesn't mean that they always feel happy with each other or have to agree about everything. If this were the case, then no family could maintain a close bond for long. Instead, there is an underlying sense of value and respect that permeates the family soil, making it a safe place to grow and learn (and even disagree).

When planting a flower, the first step is to choose good soil for your seed. If planted in hard, dry soil, your seed may die before it ever has a chance to take root. When you have found good soil, you dig a hole deep enough to protect the seed from intruders and allow it to benefit from the soil's rich nutrients.

In the same way, you want your family soil to be a nurturing and protective environment in which your children's sibling relationships can grow.

Only when deeply embedded in healthy family soil can your children's sibling relationships blossom and flourish into all God created them to be.

There are two ingredients that will help you build a climate of unity and emotional bonding into your family: family time and expressed affection. Each ingredient will promote healthy sibling relationships and can be put into practice with a surprisingly modest amount of effort. Let's take a look at each ingredient now.

FAMILY TIME

There is no substitution for positive time spent together to meld strong sibling relationships. Unfortunately, the concept of family time has been forgotten by many parents over the past decade. In contrast to the almost twenty hours the average child (ages 2–17) spends watching television each week, a miserly thirty-nine minutes are spent each week in meaningful conversation with their parents.[1] That averages out to less than six minutes a day talking about things that really matter. With quality family bonding time conspicuously absent, sibling relationships are more vulnerable to becoming strained and damaged as children go through the paces of life without regular opportunity for deep bonding and relational refueling.

Take a minute and think about your family. How much time do your children spend together, enjoying each other's company or talking about important issues in their lives? If you think there is room for improvement in this area (which is the case for most of us), then this may be one of the reasons that your children's relationships are not as close as they could be. And the rest of this chapter is just for you.

Lora and I have had a regular family time in our family ever since our children were young. While we have found ourselves getting caught up in the busyness of life and missing a week more often than I'd like to admit, we have worked hard to prioritize our goal of having our family time once a week. Both Lora and I feel that establishing our family time has been one of the best parenting decisions we have ever made. Our relationships with our children have grown closer and we have experienced wonderful times of sharing and growing together as a family that could never have happened any other way.

Our boys' sibling relationship has been positively impacted too. I have watched my boys learn to pray for others and for each other during our family times. They have learned relationship skills, such as sharing and problem solving, that have helped them handle daily living-together problems with creativity and respect. I have seen their sibling relationship develop a strong foundation that has thus far carried them through the normal aggravations of family life. I can truly say that our family times have become one of the richest experiences that I have had the privilege of being a part of.

The following is a description of how we conduct our weekly family time. Use it as a starting point as you create a family time that fits your family best. While our family time is really quite simple, it includes two important components: a fun activity and a meaningful discussion.

A Fun Activity

We either begin or end our family time with a fun activity. Just as a student pilot needs to log many hours of flight time to get a pilot's license, you want your children to log many hours of positive time together. As Stephen Covey astutely observed in *The Seven Habits of Highly Effective People,* the more deposits that people make in each other's emotional bank accounts, the more willing they are to overlook each other's shortcomings. This family activity is an opportunity for your children to invest in each other's emotional bank accounts as they share fun family experiences together. Over time, these accumulated positive family experiences of laughing and playing together will deepen your children's relationships and help offset the withdrawals that come with moments of sibling frustration.

As a child psychologist, I meet new children on a weekly basis. During our first meeting in my office, we usually talk about why they have come to see me and end by playing a game. One of the questions I always ask during our first hour together is, "What do you like best about your family?" While I have received many different answers to this question, the answer that is by far the most common is: "We do fun things together."

I further inquire about what kinds of fun things they do and get answers as varied as the children themselves. Vacations. Going on nature

FAMILY TIME ACTIVITIES

Walk through a forest preserve

Play board games

A trip to the zoo

Strolling through a shopping mall

Miniature golf

Playing volleyball with a balloon

Hitting baseballs

Going to a movie

A video rental and popcorn night

Trip to the ice cream store

Making brownies

Swimming

Bowling

Playing a computer game together

A parent vs. children basketball game

A treasure hunt

Playing at a park

walks. Eating at a favorite restaurant. Playing board games. Watching movies. Going to sporting events. The common thread that runs through each of these activities is that it is a time of meaningful family bonding.

In the past, our family times have included a variety of fun activities, some of which are included in the adjacent list.

As you can see, the possibilities for activities are endless. The only criterion we have is that we choose an activity we all enjoy. Your first family time activity can be to get together as a family and make a list of fun family time activities. As time goes on, continue to update your list as you think of new activities that you can enjoy together.

If you are just beginning regular family times and suspect that your children may not be able to successfully handle longer activities together, start with shorter activities and slowly build from there. Even if your fun activity lasts only ten minutes, that will be ten minutes of positive sibling relating and family fun that will set the stage for the next time around.

Meaningful Discussion

The second component of an effective family time is meaningful discussion. When we attended Willow Creek Community Church a few years ago, I remember hearing Pastor Bill Hybels talk about "doing life together" with his family. This phrase reflects an overall effort to purposefully walk through life together as a connected family unit. Your regular family times are a crucial part of this journey, as they give you a weekly opportunity to talk together about the important issues of life. They also help you to keep your family relationships current. To stay up-to-date on the important events in each other's lives. To rejoice together in victories and help each other in defeats. To stay connected as parents and children, siblings, and followers of Christ.

I have found that our family time discussions often fall into one of four categories:

1. Family devotions
2. Personal/family issues
3. Character traits
4. Life skills

Family Devotions

Whether reading straight from Scripture together or using any of several devotional books designed for children and families, we have found our family times to be perfect for talking about the truth in God's Word. Our family devotions include a time of reflection upon what we have read, by discussing our reactions to it and ideas for how we can apply God's truth to our lives. I particularly value these discussion times, and

FOR A LAUGH

Family Time Activities That Are NOT Highly Recommended

1. Conduct a hot-dog-eating and soda-drinking contest.
2. Spend an evening watching the newest Ultimate Fighting Championship video.
3. Have the kids wash and wax the cars while parents supervise.
4. Take a daylong trip to the Museum of Nuclear Fusion.
5. Fertilize your garden.
6. Watch a two-hour documentary on the exciting world of bacteria.
7. Go to a local restaurant and have a spit-wad fight.

love listening to my boys think through challenging issues as we talk together about how God wants us to live.

Family devotional books that you may enjoy include *Little Visits for Families* by Allan Hart Jahsmann and Martin Simon, *Kids-Life Devotions* (complied by Cook Communications), and the Heritage Builders series of family night materials, such as *Ten Commandments: Family Nights Tool Chest* or *Basic Christian Beliefs* by Jim Weidmann, John Warner, and Kurt Bruner.

Personal/Family Issues

Another type of meaningful discussion we have is staying in touch with personal and family issues. We often start by asking if anyone has an issue or subject they would like to talk about, or we go around the circle, asking each person to share one important thing happening in his life. I particularly like the activity of choosing a good question or two (or having someone else choose a question), and having us go around our family circle, taking turns giving an answer. See the list on page 39 for some of the circle questions that we have used in our family times.

As you can see, the possible questions are endless, and provide a format for discussion that moves quickly and is easy for children to engage in. There may be times when one person has a significant issue going on in his or her life, and the majority of the discussion time will be spent on talking through that issue. Regardless of the topic, your children will experience talking about important real-life issues with their family from a Christian perspective, and they will get the clear message that their thoughts and feelings are highly valued in their family.

Character Traits

A strong inner character is one of the qualities that we want our children to develop. There are many character traits you can discuss with your children, including courage, self-discipline, endurance, love, honesty, compassion, forgiveness, and respectfulness. Galatians 5:22–23 contains a wonderful list of character traits that God desires to cultivate in your family atmosphere, each of which would make an excellent family time discussion: "But the fruit of the Spirit is love, joy, peace, patience, kindness, goodness, faithfulness, gentleness and self-control. Against such things there is no law."

FAMILY TIME CIRCLE QUESTIONS

1. Name your favorite movie.
2. Name your favorite flavor of ice cream.
3. Name one thing you thank God for.
4. Name one thing you like about our family.
5. Name one thing you'd like to get better at.
6. Name one thing you are praying for.
7. Name one thing you like about the person on your right.
8. Let's all name one thing we appreciate about _____ (family member).
9. Name one important (life) lesson you have learned recently.
10. Name someone you know that we can pray for.

During one of our family times, we decided to discuss the character trait of honesty. Using an idea from *Character Builders* by Vernie Schorr, we began our discussion by having our boys take turns holding an ice cube in their closed fist, hiding it from sight. You should have seen their faces, filled with interest in our little experiment. The challenge began as they tried to keep the ice cube concealed despite the numbing, frozen sensation they felt in their hands. They slowly became aware of the futility of trying to hide an ice cube as the water began to drip through their fingers.

We then read a few passages from Scripture about honesty (Proverbs 16:11; Ephesians 4:25) and discussed why honesty is so important to God. We talked about what happens when a person is dishonest and how difficult it is to conceal a lie (the melting ice cube). We emphasized how dishonesty hurts trust and relationships. It was easy for all of us to think of times when we had been tempted to lie, but then we identified how being honest would actually work out better in the long run. The indisputable wisdom of God's Word became apparent as we wrestled through this real-life issue together.

We have had similar family time conversations about courage, compassion, respectfulness, and many other character traits. These traits are so important and woven into the fabric of life that it is good to repeat these discussions from time to time. Resources that you will find helpful in discussing character traits with your children include *Character Builders* by Vernie Schorr, and the Heritage Builders series of family night materials, including *Christian Character Qualities* and *Ready for Adolescence.*

Life Skills

As I mentioned in the Introduction, there are a wide variety of living-together skills that your children need to learn if they are going to get along with each other. In addition, there are also several skills that will help them effectively handle challenges outside the home, such as with school, peers, sports, and other life situations. The Life Skills list located at the bottom of this page, though far from exhaustive, will give you a few ideas of life skills you can discuss with your children during your family times.

The Family Time Discussion Guides found at the end of this book are perfect for teaching several living-together skills that will build healthy sibling relationships. Specific steps for teaching your children other important life skills can be found in my book *The Parent Survival Guide.*

Finally, we always end our family times with a time of prayer. We often take turns praying for each other and make sure that everyone has a chance to pray. This allows us to have the experience of bringing our requests and thanksgiving to God together as a family. It also has the benefit of giving our children the opportunity to hear Lora and me pray, thus providing them with different models of how to talk to their heavenly Father.

LIFE SKILLS

Sharing	Expressing angry feelings
Taking turns	Responding to teasing
Negotiating	Introducing yourself
Solving problems	Starting a conversation
Being inconvenienced	Good sportsmanship
Responding to failure	Handling peer pressure

As you can see, a regular family time is a powerful tool for creating a nurturing family soil in which strong sibling relationships can take root. Some of you may be realizing that you never experienced this type of family time when you were a child, and may wonder if you are capable of pulling it off. Lora and I were certainly no experts on family times when we began with our young family, but we jumped in and gave it a try. Over time, the discussions, teaching times, and family activities became more familiar and comfortable. I have found that children do not expect you to be smooth and polished; they just want to know that you care enough to invest time in them.

In his book *The Seven Habits of Highly Effective Families,* Stephen Covey tells the story of a father who felt very inadequate in his ability to lead a family time. Nonetheless, the father gave it a try and after three months of regular family meetings, wrote this:

> Growing up, my family didn't talk much except to put each other down and to argue. I was the youngest, and it seemed as if everyone in the family told me that I couldn't do anything right. I guess I believed them, so I didn't do much in school. It got so I didn't even have enough confidence to try anything that took brains. I didn't want to have these family nights because I just didn't feel I could do it.
>
> But after my wife led a discussion one week and my daughter another week, I decided to try one myself. It took a lot of courage for me to do it, but once I got started, it was like something turned loose in me that had been tied up in a painful knot ever since I was a little boy.
>
> Words just seemed to flow out of my heart. I told the members of my family why I was so glad to be their dad and why I knew they could do good things with their lives. Then I did something I had never done before. I told them all, one by one, how much I loved them. For the first time I felt like a real father—the kind of father I wished my father had been.
>
> Since that night I have felt much closer to my wife and kids. It's hard to explain what I mean, but a lot of new doors have opened for me and things at home seem different now.

CTION ONE: PREPARE THE SOIL

EXPRESSED AFFECTION

The second ingredient for creating a strong family bond is regularly expressing your affection for your children. Each one of your children wants to know that he or she is deeply loved by you. The more your children truly know this, the less they have to fight with each other for your love and attention. You don't have to fight for what you already have.

Here are two simple ways that you can let each of your children know how much you love them, and, in so doing, add to the richness of your family soil and set the stage for closer sibling relationships.

Physical Touch

Growing up in western Canada, I had not been exposed to the U.S. pastime of football, but like every other red-blooded Canadian boy, had become fully engrossed in ice hockey. After I moved to Southern California during my teens, one of my friends talked me into joining the varsity football team in my junior year of high school. The coach placed me on the offensive line. In everyday language, that means that he thought I could do the least damage as a blocker.

During my short football career, I played on only one play of one game, a kickoff, lasting all of about fifteen seconds. Somehow during my debut, I managed to slip and fall on the dewy grass before I even touched one of the opposing players. Despite my thoroughly embarrassing and dismal performance that game, I remember Coach Barry, who was built like a large section of the Great Wall of China, squeezing me on the shoulder one day as I walked to the locker room.

"Hey, Cartmell, how ya doing?" he said with a smile, looking straight at me.

It was not his friendly greeting that I remember most about that five-second locker room encounter. It was that he touched me.

I felt my heart leap. The coach had squeezed my shoulder. I knew that he didn't have to. He chose to. I also instinctively knew that the coach didn't touch just anybody. He touched the players he liked, or so I reasoned.

All of a sudden, I felt like a real player on that team. My personal stock shot up through the roof. I was included. Not only did the coach say hi to me, he knew my name, and actually went out of his way to make physical contact with me. Maybe he thought I had real potential. Maybe I wasn't as bad a lineman as I thought.

That's a lot of mileage from one touch.

How do you like it when someone, perhaps a friend or your spouse, touches you on the shoulder, arm, or hand? Do you suddenly feel more connected with and closer to that person? I recently walked up behind Lora while she was working at the computer and gently started rubbing her shoulders. Immediately, her upper body relaxed as she closed her eyes, leaned her head back, and said, "I don't want you to ever stop."

That's the power of touch.

Respectful, warm physical touch from a friend says, "I like you." When coming from a parent, it says even more: "I love you. You're important to me. I value our relationship. I'm glad you're my child." It touches the very heart of your parent/child relationship and builds it from the inside out.

How often do you touch your children?

I suggest that you make it a goal to touch *each* of your children between three and five times each day. For those of you brave souls who have a larger number of children in your family (four or more) you may have to slightly reduce the number of touches per day that you shoot for. If you look for opportunities to touch your children, you will find that they abound. As you pass in the kitchen or hallway, walk behind them while they are sitting down, help them with their homework, or sit beside them in the car, you can give them a little hug, touch, or squeeze on the shoulder, arm, elbow, knee, or hand. Other times, such as tucking them into bed or sitting together on the couch, provide an opportunity for longer periods of touch. Some children love to have their hair touched or back scratched. With a little practice, you will find that three to five touches a day will seem easy. Find the types of touch that communicate love to each of your children and engage in them regularly.

When I'm driving and our boys are in the backseat, I occasionally reach my hand behind me and lay it, palm up, on the backseat between them. They each immediately lay their hand on mine, so that all three of our hands are touching. It takes only about ten seconds, but immediately bonds us together as father and sons. It bonds them together as brothers as well, for their hands are also touching each other.

One day, our boys were playing a computer game together. I walked over to them, kissed each of them gently on the cheek, and squeezed their shoulders.

"I love both of you guys so much, and it's fun to see you playing so nicely together," I said.

"Thanks, Dad," they each replied, their eyes glued to their game.

I didn't need a bigger response. I knew I had made my point. I loved *each* of them and just wanted to make sure that they both knew it. And they did.

Verbal Reminders

I am reminded of the joke about the unhappy wife who looked at her husband of fifteen years and yelled, "You never tell me that you love me!" The husband looked back at her with a matter-of-fact expression on his face and said, "I told you I loved you when I married you. If anything changes, I'll let you know."

> **TIP:** Place four or five small stickers at various places around the house (on the refrigerator, on the entertainment center, on the computer monitor). Every time you see a sticker, immediately find each child within eyeshot and give him or her a warm squeeze or a verbal reminder of your love. It really works!

The humor in this joke lies in the fact that we all know it doesn't work that way. This wife had every reason to be upset with her husband for not reaffirming his love for her. How fortunate are those who hear those words on a regular basis. I am always astounded and saddened when I hear a mother or father tell me, usually with tears in their eyes, that they seldom heard their parents tell them that they loved them when they were children. Not surprisingly, it often doesn't come naturally for those parents to verbally reaffirm their love for their own children.

Just as you work to develop the habit of regularly touching your children, I encourage you to build the habit of telling your children that you love them. I try to tell our boys that I love them once every three or four days (not including bedtimes). While I don't always reach my goal, I keep working at it. If my life were to end tomorrow, I want our boys to know how much their father loves them. I figure regularly telling them is one good way to get that done.

It is easy to underestimate the power of our words. Not too long ago, following a lively game of basketball with our boys, Jacob looked up at me while he was putting the basketball away and said, "I sure love spending time with my dad."

Not only was I touched by this spontaneous expression of love from my son, I was taken aback by his choice of words. For about two weeks earlier, I had started using that exact phrase when I spent time with either of the boys. Following our times together, I would say, "I sure love spending time with my buddy," followed by a warm hug. Having heard me use that phrase on several occasions, Jacob had picked it up and used it to express his own feelings of affection.

Your words make more of a difference than you might imagine. With physical touch and verbal reminders, create a strong family bond by making sure that your children know how deeply loved they are.

In this step we have discussed how you can strengthen your children's sibling relationships by cultivating a strong family bond. Your children will grow closer relationships and get along better in a family soil that includes positive bonding times, meaningful family discussions, and warm parental affection.

SUMMARY: HOW TO CREATE A STRONG FAMILY BOND

1. A weekly family time
   a. A fun activity
   b. Meaningful discussion
      1) Family devotions
      2) Personal/family issues
      3) Character traits
      4) Life skills
2. Expressed affection
   a. Physical touch
   b. Verbal reminders

QUESTIONS FOR REFLECTION

1. How would you describe your family's relational soil? How did it get that way?

2. List five fun family time activities that your children would enjoy.

3. List five family time circle questions (see page 39) that would work with your children.

4. How do you think having a regular family time strengthens your children's sibling relationships?

5. Read Galatians 5:22–23; Ephesians 4:25–27; and Colossians 3:12–15, then review the list of Life Skills on page 40. Make a list of five character traits or life skills that you would like to discuss in a family time setting with your children. Why did you choose these traits or skills?

6. What obstacles might you encounter as you begin a weekly family time? How will you overcome them?

7. Were your parents openly affectionate with you when you were a child? How natural is it for you to express verbal and physical affection to your children?

8. What kind of impact do you think frequent and consistent physical and verbal affection will have on your children's sibling relationships? Why?

PRAYER SUGGESTIONS

Ask God to guide you as you initiate regular family times with your children. Also pray that God will help you build the habit of showing regular physical and verbal affection to each of your children. If you are married, remember to encourage and support each other as you begin to enrich your family soil. If you are a single parent, thank God in advance for helping you create the family soil that your children need.

1. Mr. and Mrs. Johnson have never conducted a family time with their family. How can they introduce the idea to their children?

2. Your fourteen-year-old daughter, Roxie, is not used to receiving regular physical or verbal reminders of your love for her. How can you help her become comfortable with your new way of showing affection?

   (You can find sample answers on page 229.)

Begin your family times with Family Time Discussion Guide #1: Our First Family Time.

CONNECT WITH EACH CHILD

Fourteen-year-old Alex is a blond-haired, intellectually gifted boy who tends to be shy and reserved. He enjoys spending time alone and usually has only one or two close friends at a time. When his rambunctious sister becomes too much to handle, Alex usually takes the road of less conflict and generally tries to stay out of her path.

Alex's twelve-year-old sister, Katie, on the other hand, is a whole different bag of marbles. Katie switches moods at the drop of a hat. She has always struggled with reading and can be very stubborn when she wants to get her way. Her brother's age and size do not intimidate her; in fact, Katie has an uncanny ability to find Alex's buttons and push them on a regular basis.

Or consider eleven-year-old Tiffany. She is one of those dream children (perhaps you have heard of them, or maybe even met one at one of your children's birthday parties). She loves the seventh grade, has lots of friends, and is a good athlete. A charming and likeable girl, she is very easy to be around.

Tiffany's seven-year-old brother, Connor, however, is a walking whirlwind. While his intentions are in the right place, his nonstop activity level would try the pope's patience. As a result, the stress level of the family always seems to be at its peak, and Connor is likely to be at the epicenter of any problem.

What do all these children have in common?

First, they are all very different.

Second, they are siblings.

Despite the fact that they share parents and approximately fifty percent of their genes, siblings can be as different as night and day. Or oil and water. One excels at sports; the other has average physical coordination. One excels in academics; the other struggles with reading. One is full of confidence; the other is constantly seeking approval and attention. One is a social magnet; the other alienates peers without even knowing it.

RESPONDING TO DIFFERENCES IN SIBLING TEMPERAMENT

A person's temperament refers to his overall style of relating to the world around him and is rooted in his genetic makeup. Sibling differences in temperament strongly influence the quality of sibling relationships. For instance, research has consistently found that children with difficult temperaments (e.g., emotionally intense, high activity level, impulsive, easily frustrated, cognitively inflexible) often experience high levels of conflict with their siblings, while children with moderate temperaments find it much easier to handle everyday sibling frustrations.[1]

Make a list of three words that best describe each of your children. Look at the sidebar "Personality Traits" below for ideas.

The words you chose describe your children's temperaments. The best way to identify your children's different temperaments is by watching them closely. How do they generally approach life? What is their natural way of responding to everyday frustrations? How do they interact with other children? What is their typical mood? You can often see their inborn differences from the time they are toddlers and sometimes even earlier. One child is easily frustrated by the slightest inconvenience, while another could sit happily through a tornado. One child doesn't think twice about hitting or pushing other children, while another child finds it difficult to even say hello.

PERSONALITY TRAITS

Compliant	Rowdy	Aggressive
Outgoing	Gentle	Stubborn
Strong-willed	Impulsive	Rough-and-tumble
Easygoing	Cautious	Oppositional
Soft	Daring	Intense
Loud	Mellow	Anxious
Happy-go-lucky	Sullen	Active
Finicky	Even-keeled	Moody
Argumentative	Sensitive	Good-natured

As you might imagine, children's different temperaments cause them to respond differently to sibling conflict. Strong-Willed Sandy has difficulty sharing and taking turns and usually contributes a lot of yelling and arguing to any sibling dispute. Aggressive Andy quickly resorts to name-calling and physical aggression in order to get his way. The first response of Easygoing Emily is to suggest a reasonable way to work things out. Cautious Cameron seeks to avoid conflict by giving in to his more dominant siblings or quickly running to parents for assistance.

Understanding your children's temperaments will give you important clues for how you can best help them respond to sibling conflicts. Strong-Willed Sandy needs help learning to stay calm and thinking of cooperative ways to solve problems. Aggressive Andy needs to practice using respectful words instead of hurtful words or actions. Easygoing Emily and Cautious Cameron need help standing up for themselves when their siblings try to take advantage of their more gentle natures.

TAKE INVENTORY OF YOUR CHILDREN

Once you have considered how your children differ in temperament, the next step is to think about their areas of strength and weakness. For an example of how you could do this, read through the sample Individual Child Inventory for "Henry" on the following page.

You will complete an inventory for each child during the Questions for Reflection. As you fill out and examine your Individual Child Inventories, you will find ways each of your children needs a little different care from you:

- One child needs an extra dose of physical touch and affection.
- One child needs extra help with homework organization.
- One child needs extra help meeting new friends.
- One child needs extra help with expressing angry feelings appropriately.

Different children have different needs, and it is up to you to be the parent that each of your children need. But how do you meet each of your children's individual needs without one of them feeling left out? Sibling studies have consistently indicated that children exhibit more

INDIVIDUAL CHILD INVENTORY

NAME: Henry

STRENGTHS: hard worker, good sense of humor, honest, loves God, relates well with friends

AREAS FOR GROWTH: sticking with not-so-fun tasks, learning when to stop a joke, controlling his temper, playing fairly with his brother

SITUATIONS THAT CAN BE DIFFICULT FOR HIM/HER: unsupervised sibling play, playing/joking with his brother in the car, any time he gets mad

HOW I CAN HELP:

1. Watch for signs that Henry is getting frustrated and intervene early.
2. Keep my ears open for negative behavior during unsupervised sibling play.
3. Use family time to discuss issues of (a) being considerate of others, (b) playing fairly, and (c) controlling anger.
4. Provide extra encouragement during not-so-fun tasks.
5. Watch for Henry playing positively with his brother or controlling his anger and let him know he's doing a great job!

emotional and behavioral problems when parents treat one sibling preferably to another.[2] Yet, because of their individual characteristics and needs, it is impossible to treat each of your children *exactly* the same.

One research study shed helpful light on this issue when it found that "unequal" attention from parents is only harmful to sibling relationships if the children *perceive* it as being unfair. Furthermore, the children in this study reported that their parents treated them and their siblings equally most of the time and when there was a difference in parental treatment, three-quarters of the children did not think they were being treated unfairly! Instead, they viewed the different treatment as being due to factors they considered "reasonable," such as the sibling's different ages, individual needs, or personal characteristics.[3]

What does this mean for your family? It means that with age and experience, children learn that their siblings have different needs than they do. They begin to understand that on occasion, parents need to spend extra time with one child because of the child's age or individual circumstances. It also means that in families where parents are meeting *each* child's need for love and attention, it is easier for the children to understand when a sibling needs a little extra help now and then.

Danny is an eight-year-old boy whose five-year-old brother, Kevin, is autistic. I asked Danny if his parents had to spend any extra time with Kevin because of his condition.

"Yeah, they have to spend extra time with him," Danny replied.

"What do you think about that?"

"I don't mind," Danny said, without hesitation.

"It doesn't bother you?" I probed.

"No," he confirmed, "Kevin needs it."

Danny then went on to tell me how he enjoyed helping Kevin learn his school lessons. His eyes sparkled with pride as he told me about his role of being a student teacher to his brother. While Danny and Kevin experienced the regular sibling frustrations that all brothers share, they clearly had a strong sibling relationship, despite Kevin's challenges.

Having already spoken at length with Danny's parents, I knew more than Danny thought I did. I had already learned that they took great care to spend individual time with Danny as well as with Kevin. The effect of this was abundantly evident in their son. Even with a special-needs brother who required lots of extra parental attention, Danny clearly felt loved and cared for. His parents had made sure of it.

CONNECTING WITH EACH OF YOUR CHILDREN

One of the needs that all children have is to feel connected with their parents. In his book *Breakthrough Parenting,* author and speaker John Maxwell explains that before you can *direct* your children, you must *connect* with your children. Before you can have the meaningful impact that God intends you to have on their lives, you must first make a relational connection with each of them.

The more connected you are with each of your children individually, the easier it is for them to develop healthy sibling relationships. Your strong parent/child connection gives them a solid platform from which to venture out and develop other meaningful relationships. When your children are fully connected with you, they can begin to see their siblings as friends and partners, rather than as competitors for parental affection.

Maxwell offers the following checklist of questions to help you gauge your current level of connectedness to each of your children.

1. What gives my child joy?
2. Who is my child's hero?
3. What does my child fear most?
4. Which activities give my child energy?
5. Which activities wear my child out?
6. If my child chose this year's vacation, where would he or she want to go?
7. If my child could pick one activity for me to do with him or her, what would it be?
8. What music does my child like?
9. Other than going to school or sleeping, what does my child spend the most time doing each week?
10. What does my child want to be when he or she grows up?

How many of these questions can you answer for each of your children? Your results will indicate how connected you are with each of your children right now. The more disconnected a child feels with you, the more he or she may compete with siblings to capture your attention. If you found that you were unable to answer one or more of these questions for a child, then it is time for some one-on-one time with that child. When each child feels fully connected to you, you will find that sibling cooperation and harmony is easier to attain.

Read the sidebar "Ways to Connect with Each Child" (on the following page) and choose one or two ideas to implement. Make time to get reconnected and stay connected with each of your children. Depending on their individual temperaments, some children may be more difficult to connect with than others. But each one of your children is well worth the effort, so stick with it!

WAYS TO CONNECT WITH EACH CHILD

1. Go for a walk together.
2. Have breakfast together every two weeks.
3. Regularly play a two-player game together.
4. Take turns going on a special outing (dinner and a movie) with each child.
5. Play the "What's your favorite . . . ?" game with each child. (Take turns asking each other questions about favorite things.)
6. Spend a short time together each night before bed, talking about the day and praying together.
7. Ask each child how he or she would like to spend time with you individually.

CONNECTING AS A FAMILY

Not only do you want to stay connected with each of your children individually, but you want your whole family to be connected with each other. Paul's analogy of the church functioning as a body (1 Corinthians 12) is very applicable to how God designed us to relate to each other in our families. As with our physical bodies, our family operates at its best when all our "parts" are functioning in the special way that God has created them. Staying connected with each of your children is one way to help them grow in the unique strengths and characteristics that God has given them.

But our physical bodies are much more than a collection of individual parts; they are integrated units with many different parts working together as one. In the same way, your family is comprised of individuals who are connected at the deepest level of relationship. And when your family is functioning properly, your individual "parts" will pull together as a single unit.

Not too long ago, our youngest son, Luke, became tearful at the thought of going on a school field trip without one of us tagging along.

"I might get a bit homesick," he said softly, his head lowered and lips quivering.

"Luke, you sound kind of nervous," I said.

"I'll miss you guys," Luke replied.

"Honey," Lora softly said while she gave him a reaffirming squeeze, "Miss Julie will be there and she'll stay with you the whole time. You can stand right by her."

"I know," said Luke, the tears starting to flow, "but I'll really miss you."

Jacob, who had been waiting patiently, could not stay silent another second. "Luke, I've been on lots of field trips, and I used to be nervous too, but now they're fun," he blurted out.

"Luke, would you like to hear how Jacob learned to stay calm and have fun on field trips?" I asked.

Luke sniffled. "Well, okay."

During that time, we gave Luke the extra help and attention he needed to gradually overcome his anxiety. We all rejoiced with him and expressed excitement at the bravery he was showing and the lessons he was learning. Some time later, I asked Jacob how he had felt about the attention we paid to Luke during this time.

"It was fine," he said. "I know Luke was having a hard time."

"So you feel okay about the extra time we spent helping Luke?"

"Yeah, because I get lots of time with you," came the reply.

There it is. Jacob felt comfortable with the time and attention we gave to Luke because he felt connected with us all through the process. Our connection with Luke did not result in disconnection for him.

FOR A LAUGH

How NOT to Connect with Your Child

1. Sleep in his/her room.
2. Put a five-by-eight-foot poster of you on the ceiling above his/her bed.
3. Give your child a cell phone and call him/her every hour.
4. Landscape your yard so that the tulips spell, "I love *(your child's name)*" from an aerial view.
5. On your child's birthday, sing "Close to You" (by the Carpenters) to him/her with a karaoke machine in front of all his/her friends.

When your family is functioning the way God designed it to, everybody gets the help they need when they need it. Each child feels connected and knows that he is deeply valued and loved. And each child has the assurance that when it is his turn for tough times, the same family will be there with him all the way.

Use your Individual Child Inventories to keep up-to-date on the unique needs that each of your children has. Through family times and one-on-one activities, stay connected with each of your children and current on what makes them tick. Their needs and interests will change over time, and you will need to adjust with them. But as you do, you will find that your children will connect with each other more easily when they stay fully connected with you.

QUESTIONS FOR REFLECTION

1. What are the main differences you see in your children's temperaments?

2. Complete an Individual Child Inventory for each of your children. (Use a separate paper, or photocopy and fill out the blank inventory on page 57.)

3. What is the most important thing you learned from your Individual Child Inventories?

4. How connected or disconnected do you feel with each of your children?

5. What is your greatest challenge in staying connected with each of your children?

6. Read 1 Corinthians 12:14–26. How do you think Paul's analogy of the church functioning as a body applies to your family?

7. What is one thing you can do to stay connected with each of your children on a regular basis? Make a plan that is simple and doable and commit yourself to do it.

INDIVIDUAL CHILD INVENTORY

NAME: _____

STRENGTHS:

_____

_____

_____

AREAS FOR GROWTH:

_____

_____

_____

SITUATIONS THAT CAN BE DIFFICULT FOR HIM/HER:

_____

_____

_____

HOW I CAN HELP:

1. _____
2. _____
3. _____
4. _____
5. _____

PRAYER SUGGESTIONS

Close this time with prayer, thanking God for the different characteristics that each of your children possesses. Pray that he will take each characteristic and shape it in the direction he desires for each of your children. Commit yourselves to stay connected with each of your children as a way of providing a rich and nourishing family soil for them to grow in.

PRACTICE MAKES PERFECT

Try your hand at identifying the unique aspects of different children. Given the following information for Alex and Katie, identify one possible strength, a weakness, a difficult situation, and a helpful parental intervention. There are many possible answers; see what you come up with.

1. Alex is fourteen years old. He is soft-spoken, shy, very intelligent, enjoys time alone, and has a few close friends.

   Strength: _____

   Weakness: _____

   Difficult situation: _____

   How I can help: _____

2. Katie is ten years old. She is moody, struggles with writing, and is stubborn and easily frustrated.

   Strength: _____

   Weakness: _____

   Difficult situation: _____

   How I can help: _____

   (You can find sample answers on page 229.)

For your next family time, use Family Time Discussion Guide #2: You Are a Special Part of Our Family.

ELIMINATE COMPARING, LABELING, AND COMPETITION

I wish you were *half* as neat as your brother!" Mrs. Davis commented. Mr. Hill took one look at Evan's room and shook his head with disgust. "You are the laziest kid I have ever seen!"

"Julie likes me the best. She told me she doesn't even like you," said Emily to her sister, with a superior grin.

Comparing, labeling, and competition. Like little weeds that sneak into your neatly landscaped flowerbed, these three intruders manage to find their way into every sibling relationship. They sneak in silently, slowly draining the nourishment from your family soil. And just when you think you've pulled the last one out, another one starts to grow in its place. It sometimes seems as if the quest to eliminate them is endless.

Some families are overrun with these fast-growing, weedlike intruders, making it difficult to see the flowers they eclipse in their path. If left unchecked, these insidious villains will wreak havoc on your children's sibling relationships. They will weaken family relational bonds and eat away at your children's relationships from the inside out.

The good news is that comparing, labeling, and competition do not have to be a regular part of your family life. As you will discover, they are no more than bad habits, and bad habits can be replaced with good ones. Like the lawn control expert, who comes to rid your yard of weeds and prevent their return, let's take a look at how you can eliminate each of these unwelcome guests from your family soil and protect your valuable seedlings.

COMPARING

If you wanted your children to hate each other as quickly and deeply as possible, all you would need to do is season your daily conversation

SECTION ONE: PREPARE THE SOIL

with a healthy dose of comparing. Comparing creates a me-against-you mentality. The positively compared child comes out looking like a goody-two-shoes and feels like she has to live up to a false image of who she really is. The negatively compared child feels like a loser, and settles into the role of the family black sheep. Either way, no one wins.

In my sibling workshops, I often ask the participants to complete this phrase: "Why can't you be like your _____?" They always fill in the blank correctly, enthusiastically shouting "brother" or "sister" to complete the sentence. We have all been there and know what it is like to be on either one end or the other of this type of damaging comparison.

Most parents compare in one of two ways: deliberately or accidentally. With deliberate comparing, the intent is usually a misguided attempt to motivate the underachieving child.

> Mom: "Matt, are you still working on that math sheet? Abby was finished with hers fifteen minutes ago!"
>
> Dad: "Hey, is this what you call a clean room? Have you seen how Elena cleaned her room? Maybe you should take a look!"

Can you feel the cringe of failure or the surge of resentment that wells up in the recipient of these comparisons? Not only do they not motivate your child, they result in anger and bitterness toward either the person making the comparison (you) or the one who is making him or her look so bad (the sibling).

Picture yourself working in an office setting and think about how you would feel if *you* were on the receiving end of a similar type of comparison:

> Manager: "Aren't you done with that spreadsheet yet? I had Donna's spreadsheet on my desk yesterday, and she hasn't even been working here as long as you!"

Do you feel like shouting, "Well, whoop-dee-do for Donna!" How lucky would you feel to have this particular manager to answer to every day?

Other comparisons happen accidentally, when you may not even realize you're making them. You may be congratulating Angela for a stellar report card, while David (who got mostly C's) listens from the other end of the family room and silently shrinks into the carpet, feeling like a failure. While you didn't intend your comment as a comparison, it was heard as one nonetheless.

How can you avoid these deadly comparisons that wreak havoc on your children's self-esteem and sibling relationships?

1. Focus on one child at a time.

Ask yourself what you would say if you had only one child. Without a sibling to compare your child to, you would focus on the problem she was experiencing or on her behavior. Even though you have several children, your goal is still the same: you want Johnny to do the best job that Johnny can do, not the best job that Susie can do. When you talk to Johnny, focus on these two things:

1. The situation at hand
2. The specific behavior (what he is saying or doing) that you want him to change

Example:

Brandon: "Mom, I'm done cleaning my room!"

Mom: "I don't think we're finished yet. I'd like you to pick up the toys in that corner and straighten up your desk. When you've done that, let me know." (Instead of, "Look at how neat your sister's room is. Why can't you be neat like her?")

Dad: "Okay, you guys, take your dinner dishes up to the counter."

Sam: "Okay."

Terry: "Why do *we* always have to do it?"

Dad: "In this family we all help, and I'd like you to help by bringing your dishes up here." (Instead of, "Funny, I don't hear your brother complaining about helping his family!")

Both kids: "Can we go to McDonald's?"

Mom: "Not today, guys."

Tammy: "Oh, well."

Tyler: "We never get to go anywhere fun!"

Mom: "Tyler, you're sad we're not going to McDonald's today."
(Instead of, "Tyler, why do you have to be the one who's always complaining?")

Tyler: "We don't ever go anywhere I want to go."

Mom: "Well, pal, I know it's frustrating when you really wanted to go somewhere and you can't. But I'd like you to say how you feel in a respectful way."

2. Point out each child's strengths and achievements.

Sitting in my office one evening, Paul confessed that he wasn't a natural at giving his children positive attention. As we talked further, it became clear that Paul had never received much positive attention from his parents when he was a child. Without realizing it, Paul found himself re-creating the same negative atmosphere for his own children. You can be sure that when one of Paul's children received any of his attention, the rest of the siblings felt immediate pangs of jealousy:

"Why did Dad give him a compliment and not me?"

"Dad must like him best."

"Dad never notices me."

The law of supply and demand can help us understand why this is so. When there is little available prime property in a desirable area, the price goes up. This is because the demand exceeds the supply. However, when there is more available prime property than there are buyers for the property, the price goes down. The supply exceeds the demand.

You possess a special commodity for which there is a very high demand among your children: your attention. This is because attention from you means many important things to your children:

I am loved.

I am important.

I am noticed.

I matter.

Warm, nurturing parental attention has an extremely positive effect on sibling relationships. Research tells us that when parent-child relationships are warm and affectionate, there tend to be positive relationships among siblings. However, when parent-child relationships are distant or conflicted, there is usually more sibling conflict and aggression.[1]

When positive parental attention doesn't come around very often, as was the case in Paul's family, children become jealous when a sibling gets a mom or dad's attention and they don't. However, if you provide nurturing attention on a regular basis to all your children, they learn very quickly that there is plenty of positive attention to go around. And when the supply of positive attention is enough to meet the demand, Johnny will learn that a compliment for Susie does not mean one less compliment for him. There are more than enough compliments for everybody!

Here are some examples of how you can point out your children's strengths and achievements in a way that will let them know that you notice them and lay the foundation for healthy sibling relationships:

Mom: "Jean, you did an excellent job putting the games away. Thanks."

Mom: *(later that day)* "Peter, you did a great job in your piano practicing today. You are sounding great!"

Dad: *(at the dinner table)* "We just want both of you to know how proud we are of how hard you are working at school. You guys are trying your best, even when the work gets kind of hard. Mom and I think you both are doing an excellent job! Congratulations!"

Mom: *(driving home from soccer practice)* "Cindy, you did great today in your practice! It was fun watching you play. You are really turning out to be a good soccer player, sweetie! *(Then she remembers her other children sitting in the car.)* And Ronnie, you are doing some great hitting in baseball, and Lily, I can't believe how good you are getting at reading!"

All kids: "Thanks, Mom."

Mom: "How did I ever end up with a group of such talented kids? It just must be my lucky day!"

LABELING

As parents, we know our children better than anyone else and sometimes even think we know everything they are capable of becoming. We see a flash of talent and are convinced that we have a natural pianist on our hands. Or we see a struggle with reading and fear that our child may not be college material.

When we do this, we make a tragic mistake. We assume that we can predict our children's future—what they can achieve and what they can't—based on a few instances of early behavior. It is like watching the first five minutes of a movie, then turning it off and trying to predict all the twists and turns of the plot that will follow. While you may be able to correctly guess a few themes, there will be many unexpected surprises that you never could have known.

Proof of this abounds everywhere you look. Distinguished people throughout history who were thought to have learning problems—such as Albert Einstein, Mozart, Thomas Edison, and Walt Disney—went on to accomplish amazing things. High school students who were cut from their basketball team go on to excel in professional sports (does the name Michael Jordan ring a bell?).

Early evidence indicated that these outcomes were improbable. But the early evidence was wrong! In 1 Samuel 16:7, Samuel took one look at Eliab and concluded that he would be the next king of Israel. But God corrected Samuel, saying, "Do not consider his appearance or his height, for I have rejected him. The LORD does not look at the things man looks at. Man looks at the outward appearance, but the LORD looks at the heart."

While Eliab was rejected as a candidate for king because of the condition of his heart, his younger brother David (who hadn't even been invited to the meeting) was chosen *because* of the condition of his heart. The outside evidence was misleading in both cases. It was the inner heart and character that made the difference.

The message for parents is unmistakable: Each of your children has unbelievable potential that may not be visible right now. In fact, there may even be evidence to the contrary. But don't be fooled by outside appearances. Jesse would never have dreamed in a million years that his sheep-herding, slingshot-wielding youngest son would become the greatest king Israel had ever known. In the same way, God has great plans of eternal significance for each one of your children, and who knows what those plans might be.

Your words can help to unleash your child's God-given potential or they can squelch it. When you label your children, you take the identity of a troublemaker, lazy kid, or a perfect child and, through constant repetition, cement that identity in your child's mind. You are telling him who he is, what he can and cannot accomplish, and what he is (or is not) likely to become.

The labels we place on our children are numerous. Take any skill or trait and simply define your child as being that skill or trait. The formula looks like this:

Skill/trait = My child

Here are some examples:

"Mindy is our little straight-A student."
"Gabriel is our all-star athlete."
"Britney is the smart one in the family."
"We call him Taz because he never sits still."
"Edward is going to be our preacher."
"Tina is our responsible girl. At least we have one!"

Toni regularly used negative labels such as "bad boy," "lazy," and "brat" when she talked about her son, William. I remember physically cringing the first time I heard those hurtful labels spill out of Toni's mouth as she criticized William's behavior as they sat together in my office. William immediately grew defensive and angry as he responded to his mother's caustic words. In my mind, I imagined how many other times William must have heard these words from his mother about the kind of boy he is, and what enormous cumulative effect this has had on his self-image. I immediately insisted on using respectful words and later talked to Toni about the damaging effect her words were having on her son.

In addition to the negative impact that labeling has on individual children, these harmful phrases can also damage sibling relationships. If Anthony is labeled the "family scholar," his sister Sharon may conclude that she is not very smart. If Jenny is labeled the "family musician," her sister Rebecca may assume that she has no musical talent. If Troy is regularly referred to as the "messy one" in the family, he will grow resentful when he sees his brothers make messes that go unnoticed.

These labels lead to false conclusions and sibling resentment. The fact is that both Anthony and Sharon can be good thinkers. While Jenny may be talented at music, Rebecca can also learn to play an instrument if she practices hard. And yes, Troy often leaves his room in shambles, but everyone in the family makes a mess at times.

You can avoid labeling your children by focusing the power of your words on three things:

1. Your child's *behavior*
2. Your child's *effort*
3. Your child's *potential*

By focusing your comments in these areas, you will send your children accurate messages about who they are and open doors to all the possibilities God had in mind for them before they breathed their first breath. Here are some examples of focusing on behavior, effort, and potential instead of using damaging labels:

Dad: "Billy, I don't like it when you argue when we ask you to do something." (Instead of, "Billy, you are the king of arguing! All you ever do is argue with us!")

(Positive focus: behavior)

Nicki: "Mom, I don't think I'll ever be as good at the clarinet as Susan. She's the musical one. I'm not."

Mom: "Nicki, you sound frustrated with your practicing."

Nicki: "I am. It's hard."

Mom: "Well then, you have a lot in common with all the great clarinet players, because they all felt that way sometimes too. Honey, how well you play the clarinet has nothing to do with Susan. It's up to *you* and how hard *you* practice. You can *both* be really good clarinet players if you want to." (Instead of, "You're right, Susan is a natural at music. You're really our little athlete, aren't you?")

(Positive focus: effort)

Mom: "Larry, I was disappointed when you chose to play today instead of finishing your chores. I *know* that you can be very responsible, because you have been many times before. Let's work on making a better choice next time, like I know you can. Okay?" (Instead of, "Larry, you are one of the most irresponsible boys I have ever seen!")

(Positive focus: potential)

COMPETITION

Judy is no stranger to sibling competition. She has eight-year-old twins, a boy and a girl, who are in the same grade. Both children do well at school, but each strives to outdo the other with their grades. Every spelling test and every math quiz is a competition, with one winner and one loser.

Jordan: "Ha! I got a hundred on my spelling test. What did you get?"

Emma: "None of your business."

Jordan: "Yeah, that's because you didn't get a hundred."

Emma: "I don't care. I got a perfect score on the science test and you didn't."

Jordan: "Well, at least you can do one thing right."

Emma: "Oh, you're so funny, I forgot to laugh."

Jordan and Emma were competing for the status of getting the best grades. There are many other forms of sibling status to compete for as well.

Who is the smartest?
Who is the best athlete?
Who has the most friends?
Who had the highest video game score?
Whom does the dog like the best?

As you probably know quite well, children can find almost anything to compete over. Most sibling competition has at its core the desire to reinforce one central message:

I AM SPECIAL!

The desire to feel special is not unique to children. We all want to feel special and loved. The problem is that our children often go about it the wrong way. They try to establish their sense of value by diminishing the value of their sibling. They seek to build themselves up by tearing their sibling down. In fact, the message they really are sending to their siblings is

I AM MORE SPECIAL THAN YOU!

How can you help your children feel special and loved in your family without their having to "win" at someone else's expense?

1. Reaffirm your children's true value.

Your children's value does not lie in their test scores or ability to kick a soccer ball into the goal but in the very nature of who they are. They are God's creation, knit together in their mother's womb by the very maker of heaven and earth (Psalms 139). We are reminded not to fall prey to the thinking patterns of this world but to understand our life and purpose from God's perspective (Romans 12:2). God does not place value on us because of any goodness or merit on our part but because we are his creation and he desires to be in relationship with us (Genesis 1:26–27; Ephesians 1:3–8).

Regularly emphasize to your children the value you *all* have, both to God and to each other. In your family devotions, read passages such as Psalm 139; John 3:16; and Ephesians 1:3–8 together, personalizing them to each of you and emphasizing the great extent of God's love for us and the value that he has undeservingly placed on each of us.

Such discussions will help underscore the true basis of your children's value to God and to your family. In so doing, you will help them avoid the mistake of trying to build their sense of importance by looking at their own efforts or accomplishments. Instead, their true value is most clearly seen when they see themselves through their Savior's eyes. Repeat these discussions as often as needed, reaffirming the importance and value of each of your children.

2. Redirect unhealthy competition.

When you hear your children try to build their status by demoting their siblings, immediate redirection is in order. With guidance that is

FOR A LAUGH

Ways for Eliminating Comparing, Labeling, and Competition That Are NOT Highly Recommended

1. Compare your child to a lower life form. ("You cleaned your room better than an amoeba would have.")
2. Compare your child to inanimate objects. ("That desk moves faster than you.")
3. Tell your child that you really didn't mean it when you said she was the "smart one."
4. Remind your spouse that you stopped comparing the children with each other *before* he did.
5. Tell your kids that you'll give $20 to the one who stops competing with his/her siblings first.

gentle yet firm, lead them toward finding a way to feel unique while showing respect for their siblings at the same time.

Examples:

Kelly: "I got a hundred on my test. I heard that you barely scraped by."

Tony: "Who asked you, anyway?"

Mom: "Hey, I just want to make sure that you both gave it your best effort. But even more important to me is that you encourage each other."

Trevor: "Ha ha! I whipped you again. You are never gonna beat me in basketball!"

Jeff: "Shut up."

Dad: *(gently taking Trevor aside)* "Hey, Trevor, it can be fun to win a game, but it is even more important to be a good sport to whomever you're playing with. See if you can find a way to be happy about winning and encouraging to your brother at the same time."

Julia: "Look, Fluffy came to me! She likes me the best!

SECTION ONE: PREPARE THE SOIL

Mom: "Wow! I can tell that Fluffy likes you a lot! Do you think Fluffy likes Randy too?"

Julia: "Um . . . maybe."

Mom: "Well, honey, Fluffy is special to all of us, and we call can take turns petting her. Do you know who Fluffy will be friends with?"

Julia: "Who?"

Mom: "Anyone who treats her in a friendly way. And I want both you and Randy to be Fluffy's special friends."

Julia: "Okay."

STEPS FOR ELIMINATING COMPARING, LABELING, AND COMPETITION

Comparing

Instead of comparing . . .

1. Focus on one child at a time.
   a. Focus on the problem at hand.
   b. Focus on the specific behavior that you would like to change.
2. Point out each child's strengths and achievements.

Labeling

Instead of labeling . . .

1. Focus on your children's
   a. behavior.
   b. effort.
   c. potential.

Competition

When you see unhealthy sibling competition . . .

1. Reaffirm your children's true value.
2. Redirect unhealthy competition.

70

Comparing. Labeling. Competition. Three unwelcome intruders that try to divide and conquer your children's sibling relationships. You can protect your children from these destructive forces by choosing constructive words and providing clear redirection when you see your children falling prey to these negative habits. As Solomon wrote, "Reckless words pierce like a sword, but the tongue of the wise brings healing" (Proverbs 12:18). Let your words bring wisdom and healing into your children's lives as you protect your family soil from these hurtful invaders.

QUESTIONS FOR REFLECTION

1. Do you remember your parents comparing you to your siblings? If so, what types of comparisons did they make? How did you feel about it?

2. How do you compare your children with each other? What impact do you think your comparisons have on them?

3. Read Proverbs 16:24. How often do you point out each of your children's strengths and achievements? Do you feel that you are an equal-opportunity supplier of positive comments?

4. Do you remember your parents labeling you (or your siblings) because of certain characteristics or behaviors when you were a child? What labels did they use?

5. What is one way that you have labeled your children? How can you focus on your children's behavior, effort, or potential instead?

6. Were you competitive with your siblings as a child? In what areas do you see your children competing with each other?

7. Review the examples of redirecting unhealthy competition on page 69. How can you redirect unhealthy competition when you see it with your children?

PRAYER SUGGESTIONS

Close this time with prayer, asking God to help you overcome the unhealthy habits of comparing and/or labeling that you have developed, perhaps from your own childhood. Thank God for his power to transform us, day by day, into his image. Express your gratefulness for God's help in replacing negative habits with positive new habits that will shape the way your children think about themselves and open the doors of potential that God has prepared for them.

PRACTICE MAKES PERFECT

Comparing

Come up with an appropriate comment to replace the following negative comparisons:

1. Comparison: "You're eating like a pig! Why can't you eat neatly like your brother?"
2. Comparison: "Do you ever hear your sister talking back like that? Why don't you learn a lesson from her?"

Labeling

Replace these labels with a comment on your child's behavior, effort, or potential.

1. Label: "Suzanne is our little straight-A student."
2. Label: "Tommy, you always act like such a know-it-all!"

Competition

Redirect these unhealthy competitive comments:

1. Competitive comment: "I got better grades than you."
2. Competitive comment: "Yeah! I won again! I just beat you five times in a row!"

   (You can find sample answers on page 230.)

For your next family time, use Family Time Discussion Guide #3: God Has Big Plans for You.

REQUIRE SIBLING RESPECT

Not too long ago, a friend gave me a copy of this Ann Landers column:

Dear Ann Landers,

Both my husband and I had parents who pitted their children against one another, and made it impossible for us to be close. I was determined that competitiveness would never separate my own two children when they were growing up. When their adolescent squabbling turned mean-spirited, I stepped in and helped them learn how to settle things before they destroyed each other.

This worked pretty well until one day when they were in their early teens. They had been quarreling and hurting each other all day, and I was sick of it. I became angry, and blew my top. "You must become better friends," I said, "because, God willing, you will both live a long time. I will be gone, and your father will be gone, and all your teachers and many of your friends will be gone. There may be only the two of you left, and you will remember what you were like as children.

"Nobody else will remember the Christmases you had, the tree house you built, the day you learned to ride a bike, the fun you had trick-or-treating, the teacher you loved in the third grade, and the kittens born in the laundry. There will be only the two of you, and you had better love each other now, because sixty years from now, only you will remember all the wonderful experiences you shared, and those memories will be golden."

They both became very quiet, and I thought perhaps they were too young to understand. But it must have made an impression, because they never squabbled or tried to hurt each other after that. I wish my parents had explained to my sister and me forty years ago that sibling rivalry is natural but brothers and sisters who are not good to each other lose something precious.

Lucille in St. Louis

What were the siblings doing that troubled this mother so much? Quarreling. Squabbling. Hurting each other. In a phrase, showing a lack of respect for each other.

As was the case for Lucille in St. Louis, we all want our children to be good to each other. We want them to get along, and more than that, to be friends. To want to stay in contact with each other beyond obligatory holidays once they have moved out of the house.

Ironically, this is one thing that you cannot guarantee will happen.

If you would like evidence of this, consider how many adults you know who have grown up without a close relationship with one or more of their siblings. When I ask how many people have distant relationships with their adult siblings in my workshops, I am always saddened to see the number of hands that are raised.

At that point in the workshop, I often pick two women from the audience and ask their names. Let's say their names are Ann and Jill. I double-check to make sure that Ann and Jill do not know each other.

"Ann," I ask, "do you think I can make you and Jill become best friends?"

"No," Ann quickly responds.

"Well, what if I threw in something nice, like some chocolate, or maybe a new pair of shoes?" I continue. The audience chuckles, seeing the futility in my efforts.

"No, you couldn't do it." Ann holds her ground.

As we go back and forth, it becomes clear to everyone that there is no way that I can externally force Ann and Jill to become best friends.

We all know why that is true. Friendship is something that is earned, not forced. We voluntarily give that place of honor in our lives to those who earn it, whether they are related to us or not. If a sibling earns it, then a close relationship will follow. If a sibling does not earn it, then a close relationship will not follow.

So, what can you do? Must you sit idly and watch your children's relationship swirl down the drain in slow motion?

Absolutely not.

Ask yourself this question: In what environment is a close sibling relationship most likely to develop? A hostile and aggressive environment? One where a sibling gets away with murder (at the other's expense) on

74

a regular basis? One where name-calling, teasing, and hitting are the norm?

Probably not.

There is one word that characterizes the environment that can best foster close sibling relationships.

Respectful.

Children are far more likely to want to become friends with a sibling who regularly treats them respectfully than with a sibling who regularly insults, hits, and teases them. In fact, most of the behaviors that result in sibling conflict can be directly linked to a lack of respect. Teasing. Name-calling. Using a sibling's possessions without permission. Put-downs. Not stopping when a sibling asks you to stop. Ignoring. Physical aggression.

All of these are disrespectful behaviors. If you had an acquaintance who regularly treated you this way, chances are you would not be inviting him or her home to dinner anytime soon. Similarly, a family environment where these behaviors run rampant is a place where sibling relationships will wither and die, not flourish and grow.

THE FAMILY RESPECT RULE

You can require that your children treat each other respectfully. As I talk with parents in my daily work, I find that an incredible amount of disrespectful behavior goes on every day between their children. Worse yet, this behavior often goes unaddressed, sometimes even unnoticed, within the everyday commotion of herding everyone into the car and getting the daily homework done.

One way to bring the issue of respect to the forefront for your children is to establish the Family Respect Rule. The rule goes as follows:

The Family Respect Rule
Everyone in our family needs to treat everyone else respectfully.
All the time.

The reason that this family respect rule is so important is that it sets the standard for how people are to treat each other in your family. It clearly states that there is *never* a time when treating another person disrespectfully is acceptable. Period. No matter what time of day, who said what, who went into whose room, or who used whose things without asking.

The biblical truth that undergirds this rule of respect is that every person in your family was created by God and is of great value to him. Jesus' death on the cross testifies to the value that God has bestowed on each of us. It is God's intention that we treat each other respectfully, not that we hurt each other with our words or actions. We are commanded to clothe ourselves with compassion, kindness, humility, gentleness, and patience (Colossians 3:12). That list leaves no room for disrespect.

As persons created by God, all of you are valued and important members of your family. You want to have a family that has fun together, enjoys each other's company, and walks as a close-knit group through the joys and trials of life. This kind of family (and sibling) bonding will *only* happen in an environment that places a high value on respect.

Each person in your family can be expected to learn (over time) to handle things that don't go their way and to express their thoughts and feelings in a respectful way. This is not to say that there will not be mistakes; indeed there will. The Family Respect Rule is the ideal, the goal you are working towards. None of us will ever accomplish it perfectly all of the time. But when it is broken, everyone knows that the problem is not that a person felt angry but that he or she chose to express feelings or handle a situation in a way that violated a valuable family relationship.

DEFINING RESPECTFUL BEHAVIOR

In Aretha Franklin's hit song "Respect," she belts out the following lyrics in her classic R&B style: "R-E-S-P-E-C-T, find out what it means to me." You need to help your children learn *exactly* what respectful behavior is and *exactly* what it is not.

Eric is a ten-year-old boy that I once worked with who was smart, energetic, and generally fun to be around. However, Eric's five-year-old brother, Alan, and nine-year-old sister, Molly, did not greatly appreciate his quick temper. While all three children could get along well at times, Mr. and Mrs. Hamilton wanted each of them to learn to treat each other more respectfully.

After discussing the Family Respect Rule with Eric and his family one session, I asked everyone what kind of family they wanted to have. After all, it was their family, and they had the power to make it whatever they wanted it to be.

"Well, what do you guys think of the Family Respect Rule?" I asked.

"I like it," said Molly, full of enthusiasm.

"Me too," Eric agreed, while Alan nodded his head.

"Sounds good to us," Mr. and Mrs. Hamilton confirmed.

"Okay. Well, how about if we make a list of what you would like your family to be like," I suggested. "After all, it is your family. Let's go around in a circle and I'll write down whatever you say." Here is the list they came up with:

The Kind of Family We Want	
Responsible	Fun
Happy	Respectful
Active	All get along

As we talked about their list, we all agreed that it sounded great. We then set upon the task of figuring out how they could make their family more like the words on that list. We decided that the Family Respect Rule might help, because a family where everyone treated each other respectfully would have a better chance of accomplishing this goal than a family where people treated each other disrespectfully.

"Well, how about if we make a list of disrespectful behaviors that could keep your family from becoming the family you want it to be," I suggested. "Then, you'll know what kind of things not to do."

"Excellent idea," Mr. Hamilton agreed.

We went around in a circle, with everyone offering one example of a disrespectful behavior. After a couple of times around the circle, here's what they came up with:

Disrespectful Behaviors	
Swear	Scream
Yell	Hit or push
Name-calling	Ignore
Hurtful comments	Walk away when someone is talking

We then proceeded to make a list of respectful behaviors that they wanted to see more often in their family. This was a fun list to make, and everyone enjoyed adding items to the list. When we were done, the list looked like this:

Respectful Behaviors

Stay calm.
Look at the person talking.
Listen to the person talking.
Talk respectfully (words, volume).
Share.
Offer to help.
Be polite.
Think of a solution instead of just getting mad.
Let the other person go first.

Once we had our definitions, everyone was clear on our objective: To reach our goal (List 1) by reducing disrespectful behavior (List 2) and by increasing respectful behavior (List 3). We were then able to identify situations in which disrespectful behavior occurred and practice treating each other respectfully instead.

There are many different ways you can define respectful behavior for your family. In *The Family Manager*, author Kathy Peel shares what her

---

JOHNSON FAMILY RULES

Do's	Don'ts
We obey God.	No yelling.
We listen to our parents.	No name-calling.
We talk respectfully to each other.	No hitting.
We listen when others are talking.	
We respect each other's stuff.	
We help each other.	
We protect each other.	

---

family calls "The Peel Team Big Ten House Rules." Here are the rules for Kathy's family:

1. We're all in this together. The team rules apply to everyone— even Mom and Dad.
2. No yelling at anyone.
3. Calling names or making unkind, cutting remarks to each other is strictly out of order.
4. Take responsibility for your own actions and words.
5. Keep confidential what you share with each other.
6. Ask forgiveness when you have hurt or offended someone, even if it was an accident.
7. Respect each other's space.
8. Respect each other's stuff.
9. Agree to abide by a family chore system.
10. Agree to get together regularly for family team meetings.

If you look carefully, you will notice that six of these ten rules relate directly to the issue of respect, while the other four are indirectly related to respectful behavior.

Some families have found it helpful to write up a family constitution or make a list of basic family do's and don'ts that they can refer back to. The sidebar "Johnson Family Rules" on the previous page gives an example of what this might look like.

However you choose to define respectful behavior for your family, you immediately make the task of responding to sibling conflicts fifty percent easier. Your task is no longer figuring out who did what first— that no longer matters! All that matters is who was respectful and who was not. The child who handles sibling conflict respectfully will reap the rewards of respectful behavior. The child who handles sibling conflict in a disrespectful way will learn that disrespectful behavior does not pay off.

LEADING YOUR CHILDREN TOWARD RESPECT

Lee Iacocca took over the reins of the Chrysler corporation in 1978 and through his wise leadership was able to save the company from bankruptcy and transform it into a successful leader in the automotive industry. Well aware of the principles of effective leadership, Iacocca is said to have wisely observed, "As goes the leader, so goes the team." In fact, he demonstrated his own commitment to his organization during its most difficult times by reducing his salary to $1 a year. As the leader, he put his money where his mouth was. Iacocca knew that organizational change begins in only one place.

> **REMINDER:** Watching you handle the challenges of parenting in a respectful way will be the greatest lesson in respectfulness your children will ever see.

At the top.

As you teach your children the importance of treating each other respectfully, they will instinctively look to you for leadership in this area. You will determine what they find.

Dad: *(shouting)* "Hey, you two! I said to knock it off!"

Peter: "He started it! He spit at me!"

Dad: "What! Danny, get over here! *(Grabs Danny by the arm and pulls him away.)* Let me spit at you and see how you like it!"

Katherine: "You didn't ask to come into my room, so get out."

Emily: "What's the big deal? I was just looking at your goldfish."

Katherine: *(shouting)* "I said get out!"

Mom: *(yelling)* "What is wrong with you two? You sound like you are both two years old! Maybe I should put you back in diapers and make you take a nap! Or better yet, I'll tape-record you and let you hear how stupid and petty you sound. If you can't learn to talk like human beings, keep your mouths shut!"

Do you feel the disrespect surging forth from these parents' responses? Remember that the Family Respect Rule applies as much to you as it does to your children. Your children are acutely aware of this. There is no room for you to be disrespectful one moment and then ask your children to be respectful the next. Children can smell the hypocrisy in that a mile away.

As your children experience you treating them with respect, despite your frustration with their behavior, they will learn firsthand how respect really looks in action. They will feel the results of respectful behavior and see benefits that come from obeying God's Word. By following the Family Respect Rule, you will create a family soil that is safe for everyone and that will set the stage for positive sibling relationships. Just as your children are responsible for their own behavior and can choose to be respectful, so can you. And before they will, you must.

TEACHING RESPECTFUL BEHAVIOR

Here are six practical steps for teaching your children how to treat each other respectfully. You can practice these steps with your children using the Family Time Discussion Guide that corresponds with this chapter. The steps are simple and each step naturally leads to the next.

Use these steps in your family times as often as you need to. There will be many colorful family discussions and role-plays that you will have around the issue of respect. Work through these steps together, using situations where your children have treated each other disrespectfully in the past. You will teach your children that they are valuable to God and valuable to your family. And things of value are worth taking care of. With each of these discussions and rehearsals, your children

SIX STEPS FOR TEACHING RESPECTFUL BEHAVIOR

1. Discuss the importance of treating each other respectfully.
2. Introduce your children to the Family Respect Rule.
3. Define disrespectful behaviors (that you want less of) and respectful behaviors (that you want more of).
4. Identify situations in which your children treat each other disrespectfully.
5. Role-play those situations, having your children practice responding respectfully.
6. Identify how handling the situation respectfully brought a positive outcome.

will gradually improve their skills at handling sibling conflicts in a respectful way. Over time, you will begin to see your children display these skills in real-life situations. When you prioritize respectfulness in your family, your children will reap the benefits, both now and in the years to come.

QUESTIONS FOR REFLECTION

1. If you have siblings, how would you describe your current relationships with them? How did respectful or disrespectful behavior play a part?

2. Would you describe your children's sibling relationships as primarily respectful or disrespectful?

3. What do you think about the Family Respect Rule?

4. Make a list of words that describe how *you* would like your family to be.

5. Read Colossians 3:12–14. Notice that the word *disrespect* is not included in the list in verse 12. Are you disrespectful to your spouse or children on occasion? If so, how?

6. What disrespectful behaviors would you like to see take a permanent leave of absence from your family?

7. For each disrespectful behavior on the previous list, identify a respectful behavior that can take its place.

8. Read through the Six Steps for Teaching Respectful Behavior. How do you think your children will respond to them?

PRAYER SUGGESTIONS

Close this time with prayer, asking God to guide you as you teach this important lesson of respect to your children. Just as important, ask God to shape you into the leader he designed you to be and to help you give your children a living model of what being respectful really looks like.

PRACTICE MAKES PERFECT

Identify a respectful parental response to the two examples given on page 80.

1. Dad: "Hey, you two! I said to knock it off!"

Peter: "He started it! He spit at me!"

Dad: _____

2. Katherine: "You didn't ask to come into my room, so get out."

Emily: "What's the big deal? I was just looking at your goldfish."

Katherine: "I said get out!"

Mom: _____

(You will find sample responses on page 230.)

For your next family time, use Family Time Discussion Guide #4: The Family Respect Rule.

PLANT THE SEED

IMPROVE SIBLING COMMUNICATION

Proverbs 15:1 tells us, "A gentle answer turns away wrath, but a harsh word stirs up anger." Jason had overlooked this important little verse when he took his sister to task for eating the last donut after school one day.

> Jason: "Hey! Who ate the last donut?"
>
> Bailey: "I did."
>
> Jason: "That was mine! Dad said I could have it!"
>
> Bailey: "I didn't hear him say that. Calm down, it's only a donut."
>
> Jason: *(slamming his fist on the counter)* "That was my donut! You shouldn't have taken it. It was my favorite kind! I've been looking forward to it all day!"
>
> Bailey: "Well, you should get a life if that's all you think about."
>
> Jason: "Shut up! It's your fault! You big pig! *(makes snorting noises)* You probably inhaled it in one bite."

Jason attacking his sister and calling her names. Bailey responding with sarcasm and indifference toward her brother's situation. This conversation quickly eroded into a disrespectful argument because of both children's poorly developed communication skills.

WHEN COMMUNICATION GOES BAD

Communication is the act of sending information from one person to another. Our words are the containers the information is sent in. The words we choose, and how we deliver them, can cause the information to reach its destination in good condition. Or, our words can damage and distort the information, resulting in hurt and angry feelings on the part of the recipient.

It is not only the words our children choose that disrupt the communication process but also the way they treat each other's words. A sibling argument, for example, is often the result of two children who both want to be listened to, but neither of them want to listen to the other person. They are, in essence, going back and forth, saying, "You be quiet and listen to me!" "No, you be quiet and listen to me!"

Sean and Jack were constantly fighting with each other. As we talked together in my office one afternoon, I asked them why they had such trouble getting along.

"He always tells me to shut up," Sean complained.

"Yeah, well, he's always shouting and swearing at me!" Jack fired back.

They each instinctively knew that their communication was a major part of the problem, but neither of them had a clue as to how to turn it around.

If children communicate negatively with each other on a regular basis, it will take its toll on their sibling relationships. Poor communication skills take an insignificant issue and transform it into a catastrophic blowout. Hurtful words, sarcastic jabs, and cruel teasing leave a burning trail of resentment and anger that can smolder for days, weeks, or even years.

On the other hand, effective communication skills take a seemingly difficult problem and quickly break it down to size. I once heard the story of a baseball player who was having dinner with his wife when their young baby began to cry. The wife was tired from a busy day of caring for an infant, so she asked her husband to change the baby's diaper. He said, "I'm a baseball player. I don't know how to change a baby." Not about to let her husband get off the hook so easily, the wife simply put it in terms he could understand. "Listen," she said, "you lay the diaper out like a diamond, you put second base on home plate, put the baby's bottom on the pitcher's mound, hook up first and third, and slide home underneath. And if it starts to rain, the game isn't called. You start all over again." Now that's effective communication!

FOUR SKILLS FOR EFFECTIVE COMMUNICATION

As author Patrick Morley wrote in *Ten Secrets for the Man in the Mirror*, we often have to do what we don't want to do to become what we want to be. This has never been more true than in the area of communication skills. For most of us, effective communication skills don't come naturally. We have to work at them.

Baby Blues comic strip authors Rick Kirkman and Jerry Scott provided a memorable example of how difficult good communication can be for children when they depicted an upset little girl staring down at her younger brother. "Hammie, you, you, you . . . ," she stammered with frustration. The mother happened upon this scene and quickly reminded her daughter, "Zoe, remember what I told you, if you can't say something nice to somebody, don't say anything at all." "Okay," the little girl reluctantly replied. Then, after thinking for a couple seconds, she looked at her younger brother and said, "Your nose looks less boogery than usual today."

Once you have made an effort to prepare your family soil, it is important to place the right seed in it. One of those seeds is the habit of effective sibling communication. Solomon wrote, "Pleasant words are a honeycomb, sweet to the soul and healing to the bones" (Proverbs 16:24). There are four skills for effective communication that will help your children learn to communicate more respectfully with each other. Each skill will be the focus of one Family Time Discussion Guide. Keep in mind that these skills will take time and practice, but will be worth every second of effort. Here is a description of each of the four skills.

1. Say the behavior you don't like and how it causes a problem.

When children get angry, they often resort to name-calling and cruel comments. To prevent this, you must teach them a more effective and respectful first response when they get aggravated. An excellent first response to sibling frustration is for your children to say the behavior they don't like and to say how it creates a problem for them. This way they are focusing on the problem *behavior*, instead of attacking their sibling. Here are two simple sentences that will help them do this:

> "When you _____ *(name the behavior you don't like)*,
> I feel _____ *(say how you feel)*."
> "When you _____ *(name the behavior you don't like)*,
> then _____ *(say how it is a problem for you)*."

If done in real life, this does not sound as strange as you might think. For instance, when Dean is upset because it is Joseph's turn to choose the video to watch one evening, he could say to his mother, "When Joseph got to pick the movie for tonight, I felt kind of sad," instead of saying, "Joseph always gets his way. He's such a crybaby!"

When Laura noisily bursts into Arthur's room without knocking, Arthur could say, "Hey, when you come into my room without knocking, it makes it hard for me to get my homework done," instead of saying, "Can't you see I'm working? Get out of here!"

Teaching your children to identify the problem behavior and say how it causes a problem for them is an excellent substitute for verbal attacking and is the first step toward productive communication and a quick resolution of the sibling conflict.

2. Take turns talking.

W. Steven Brown once said, "Communication does not begin with being understood, but with understanding others." One of the quickest ways to stop an argument cold in its tracks is for one person to be willing to listen to the other. In order for this to happen, the two people must be willing to take turns talking and listening. Now, let's face it. This is not something that most children like to do. Particularly when they are in the middle of a conflict. In fact, this communication skill is often difficult for child and adult alike.

Effective communication is similar to a friendly tennis volley, where the players take turns hitting the ball back and forth over the net. This is how tennis players warm up with each other before a match. It is not hard-core competition, where each player is trying to defeat the other. Instead, the goal is to hit the ball so that the other person *can* return it. Back and forth, with each person hitting the ball and then allowing the other person a chance to send it back.

This is the style of communication that you want your children to develop. Stating their thought or view in a respectful way and then pausing to listen to the other person's response. Back and forth, like a friendly tennis volley. One person talking, the other person listening.

3. Suggest a solution.

After your children have stated the problem and listened to each other's point of view, it is time to switch the focus from the problem to the solution. One of the reasons that arguments last so long and become so heated is that both children are stuck on the problem, just like a tire stuck in a muddy ditch. And with all that energy going nowhere, it doesn't take long before the mud starts to fly.

The way to solve this problem is to get the discussion headed in a positive direction. In Step Six, you will learn how to teach your children an effective way to find a good solution to any sibling problem. And when your children put their energy into finding a solution that will work for everyone, problems have a way of getting worked out.

Not too long ago, my two sons were watching TV while sitting on each end of our couch, with their feet congregating in the middle. As was bound to eventually happen, their feet became tangled and they started kicking each other. Realizing what was happening, I put down my book, walked over, and turned off the TV.

"Boys," I said (now that I had their attention), "if you would like to watch TV, then I'd like you to figure out how to sit on the couch together without annoying each other with your feet."

I turned around, quietly sat down, and watched them, curious as to how they would respond. Having learned that resistance would be futile, they decided not to continue arguing but to put their energy toward finding a solution. Within ninety seconds, they had it worked out.

"Okay, Dad," Jacob excitedly said, "we're done. Look, Luke can put his feet in front and I can put mine in the back. See, we're not touching!"

There had been no shouting. No arguing. Just working together to find a solution. I congratulated both of them on a problem well solved and gave them each a high five. Oh, yes, and I turned the TV back on.

4. Watch out for hazards.

Just as a washed-out bridge will ruin your Sunday afternoon drive, communication hazards will shut down your children's effective communication in a hurry. Respectfulness is the key for effective sibling

FOR A LAUGH

Five Signs That Your Children's Communication Skills Need Improvement

1. You consider it a good day when they commit less then ten communication hazards. Each.
2. Your children interrupt each other while they are still interrupting each other.
3. You can't tell your children's voices from each other unless they're shouting.
4. Your children's idea of "taking turns talking" is pausing to catch their breath.
5. You discover that your children can call each other names in sign language.

communication, and, as we learned in Step Four, it is the standard that your children must work toward and be held accountable to.

Keep in mind that no child can be expected to communicate angry or hurt feelings perfectly every time, and there will be times when your children may blow a gasket and say hurtful things they really don't mean. Any parent of a teenager can attest to that. In these instances, your job is to try to understand their intense feelings and help them to communicate those feelings in a more productive way. However, these extreme instances should be the exception, not the rule. If you find that your children experience intense feelings of anger or sadness often, you should immediately consult with a qualified therapist for additional guidance.

Your general expectation is for everyone in your family to learn to express their feelings in a respectful way. Some children will master this more quickly than others, but everyone can be expected to be moving in the same direction. Review this list of communication hazards with your children and make sure they know that each one is off-limits:

1. Yelling
2. Name-calling

3. Sarcasm
4. Put-downs
5. Teasing
6. Hurtful comments
7. Using a disrespectful tone of voice

It is important for your children to learn to express their emotions, even very strong emotions, in a respectful way that does not attack other people or violate family relationships. "I hate you and wish you were dead!" and "I am furious at you for telling my friends about my birthmark!" both communicate extremely strong emotions. However, the second statement contains an element of self-control and expresses important feelings without verbally trying to hurt the other person. With time and practice, your children can learn to communicate even the most difficult of emotions in a respectful way.

TEACHING EFFECTIVE COMMUNICATION SKILLS

Having read through these four skills for effective communication, there are a few thoughts that may be surfacing in your mind right now.
"Yeah, right."
"Like my kids are going to talk that way."
"There's no way my kids are going to do that stuff."
You're right. These communication skills are very difficult and they don't come naturally to most of us. In fact, many children never become skilled at communication and take their poor communication skills with them into adulthood and into their marriages. These skills run counter to your children's basic instinct to lash out in anger and call each other names. So, how can you build these effective communication skills into their young repertoires?
You have to teach them.
And if you do your job at teaching, your children can do their job at learning. Most children are very capable of learning positive communication skills, if given the right instruction, encouragement, and opportunity for practice. There are two approaches you can use to teach your children these valuable communication skills so that they can use them in real life.

The first approach is to teach them in your family times, using the Family Time Discussion Guides included at the end of this book. You will need to practice each skill several times for your children to become comfortable using them, so review the skills as often as you need to. As you practice these communication skills together as a family, your children will begin to have them at their disposal when a real-life conflict arises. This sets you up for the second method of training: on-the-spot.

ON-THE-SPOT TRAINING

While your children are becoming more skilled at communicating respectfully, they will still need reminders from you when the going gets tough. On-the-spot training occurs when you catch your children either in or before a conflict and help them to apply their new skills right then and there.

Before the Problem Begins

One chance for on-the-spot training occurs when you see a sibling conflict developing on the horizon. Before there is a chance for things to get out of hand, remind your children to use their new communication skills. Any of the following sentences will increase your children's chances of handling the situation positively:

> Parent: "Kyle and Deanna, I want you to use the skills we've been practicing."
>
> Parent: "Who's going to listen to the other person first?"
>
> Parent: "Deanna, if Kyle did something you don't like, tell him what he did and how it makes a problem for you."

As the result of your reminder, your children's memories are triggered and they have a better chance of using the skills that you have been practicing together. The more you have discussed and rehearsed these communication skills, the more easily they will come to your children when they really need them.

Help Them Make a U-Turn

A second way to do on-the-spot training is when your children are in the middle of a conflict and have obviously forgotten every positive communication skill they have ever learned. Unless their communication has become negative enough to warrant immediate separation or time-outs, you can help your children turn this crash-and-burn argument into a productive discussion.

When your children are locked in a negatively spiraling argument, immediately interrupt them and take an active role in helping them to get things back on track. Depending on which communication skill you think would be the most helpful for the situation, actively guide your children in putting that skill to work. Here's how you can help them make a U-turn for each of the four communication skills:

1. Say the behavior you don't like and how it causes a problem.

Parent: "Hey, wait a second. Deanna, if you're angry at Kyle, I'd like you to tell him what he did and then how that causes a problem for you. And please do it respectfully."

2. Take turns talking.

Parent: "Whoa, guys, this is getting out of hand. How about if one person talks and one person listens. Kyle, I'd like you to listen to Deanna first."

3. Suggest a solution.

Parent: "You guys are both stuck on the problem. How about if you start thinking of possible solutions that will work for everyone. Kyle, what is one possible solution?"

4. Watch out for hazards.

Parent: "Hey, Deanna, that was very disrespectful. You both need to work this out respectfully. Remember, being disrespectful will just get you sent to time-out. Figure out how to say what you think respectfully. If you need help, just ask me."

Family time rehearsal and on-the-spot training are essential if you want your children to learn how to communicate respectfully and effectively with each other. These skills are difficult and will take time to learn. This is why, in addition to practice, it is critically important for your children to see how you put them into action yourself.

SETTING THE RIGHT EXAMPLE

Children learn to communicate respectfully by practicing effective communication skills and by observing effective communication skills in action. It is your job to show your children how to do it right. Remember, change begins at the top, and that means you.

There are 6,570 days from a child's birth until they turn eighteen. These are your days of most significant influence on your children. Your children see you communicate many times each day, which means they will observe your communication style literally tens of thousands of times during the eighteen years you are together. If the majority of what your children hear from you during this time is negative communication toward them or your spouse, their ability to learn these valuable communication skills will be severely impaired. Instead, your children will soak up the bad habits they have seen from you hundreds, maybe thousands of times.

Vicki is a mother who recently reminded me of the incredible influence parents have on their children. As we talked together in my office, she told me that in her frustration she often ended up yelling at her children and had a hard time keeping her cool when they misbehaved. As we talked further, Vicki told me about the heated environment she grew up in as a child, where both of her parents frequently shouted and made hurtful comments to the children and to each other when they were angry. As she described the family atmosphere in her childhood home, it became clear to both of us that she was carrying these hurtful relational patterns into her own home and her children were beginning to learn them as well. Fortunately, I was able to remind Vicki that she had the power to break this harmful family cycle, and the first step was to show her children a new way of relating to each other.

As you teach and rehearse these communication skills with your children during your family times, let them see you put them into practice as well. The impact of your healthy example can shape their lives forever. As Paul Harvey once said, "We expect our leaders to be better than we are . . . and they should be—or why are we following them?" There is no one that your children are watching more closely or following more intently than you. As Paul encouraged the Corinthian believers to "Follow my example, as I follow the example of Christ" (1 Corinthians 11:1), let your example be one that teaches your children to communicate with each other in a way that is respectful, honors God, and builds healthy family relationships.

SUMMARY

Four Skills for Effective Communication

1. Say the behavior you don't like and how it causes a problem.
2. Take turns talking.
3. Suggest a solution.
4. Watch out for hazards.

Teaching Effective Communication Skills

1. Family time rehearsals
2. On-the-spot training
   a. Before the problem begins
   b. Help them make a U-turn

QUESTIONS FOR REFLECTION

1. How would you describe your communication style?

2. Which of the Four Skills for Effective Communication do your children need to work on the most?

3. Which hazards do your children commit most often? Which do you commit?

4. How quickly do you think your children can learn these important communication skills *without* using family time rehearsals? How will these rehearsals help your children learn these valuable skills?

5. What is one situation where on-the-spot training will be helpful for your children?

6. Read 1 Corinthians 11:1. How can you use your example to teach your children to communicate the way God wants them to?

PRAYER SUGGESTIONS

Ask God to help you learn to communicate with your children in a way that models healthy communication in every situation. As you pray, emphasize the importance of your role as the family leader, and commit yourself to lead your children toward communication that honors God and builds your family.

PRACTICE MAKES PERFECT

1. Using these new communication skills, think of a better way a child could communicate these thoughts:

   "You're always bugging me! I wish I never had a brother!"
   "You are such a brat!"

2. Seth and Lucy are taking turns playing a computer game. All of a sudden, you hear shouting from the computer room. What would you say to intervene on the spot in this situation?

   (You will find sample responses on page 231.)

For your next family time, use Family Time Discussion Guide #5: Say It the Right Way, Right Away.

STEP TOWARD SOLUTIONS

Michael is a blond-haired, nine-year-old boy I once worked with who had developed a habit of punching his seven-year-old brother when he was angry at him.

"Michael," I asked, "when you get mad at Daniel, what would be a better thing to do than hit him?"

Michael thought for a moment. "I don't know," he said.

"Take a minute," I encouraged him. "See what you can come up with."

Michael thought for about ten additional seconds. "Yell at him," was his reply.

I also worked with Ellen, a tall thirteen-year-old girl who frequently complained about her nine-year-old sister, Anna. Every session, Ellen would complain about how difficult Anna was to live with.

"When you get mad at Anna," I asked in one of our first sessions, "what is the best way you can think of to handle it?"

"I could ask her to stop," Ellen replied.

"Hey, that might work," I said, encouraged that she had identified a positive solution. Wanting to see if she could take it to the next step, I continued. "But let's say that Anna kept on doing something that bothered you. What would you do then?"

"I don't know," Ellen said. "I'd probably hit her."

"You sure?" I asked.

"Yup," she said.

"Final answer?"

"Final answer."

Both Michael and Ellen lacked the ability to quickly come up with good solutions when faced with a sibling problem. To their credit, this is not always easy to do. But it is a skill that they must learn if they want to solve sibling conflicts in a productive way.

WHAT ARE THEY FIGHTING ABOUT?

In some families, siblings fight more than you might think. One sibling study found that preschool children with younger siblings experience conflict an average of seven times an hour, with a quarter of those conflicts resulting in either verbal or physical aggression.[1] Another study found that nine- and ten-year-old siblings reported an average of 4.7 fights per day, with fights lasting an average of 8.1 minutes each. The children remained angry or upset for an average of 5.8 minutes after the fights were over. It is encouraging to note that these same children reported cooperating and having fun with their siblings an average of 9.2 times each day—nearly twice as much as they fought![2]

I have made a habit of asking the siblings I work with what they fight about the most. Three of the most common responses I get are sharing, taking turns, and the other sibling "bugging me." This is similar to the results of a study that identified the most common reasons for sibling fighting among fourth- and fifth-grade children as being in a bad mood, getting even, and protecting their room or toys. Gaining parental attention was listed as the least common reason that these children fought with each other![3] Other research on sibling behavior found that "realistic conflict" over everyday issues actually accounted for more sibling fighting than did the concept of "sibling rivalry."[4]

The bottom line is that siblings fight over everyday issues. Who gets to use the computer first. Who gets to sit in the front seat. Who used my toys without asking. As we have previously pointed out, this is due, in large part, to the fact that their living-together skills still need developing, which includes their ability to respectfully and cooperatively work through problems together. But does improving children's problem-solving skills really reduce sibling conflict?

The answer is yes. Several studies have demonstrated the effectiveness of teaching problem-solving skills in reducing sibling conflict.[5] One study found that when families used problem-solving steps together, the sibling relationships improved, *even if one or more of the children had a difficult temperament!*[6] That's worth the price you paid for this book right there. Another study found that children who used problem-solving, negotiation, and positive communication skills to solve conflicts showed less destructive behaviors (such as yelling, name-calling, hitting, withdrawing) and reported warmer sibling relationships. Siblings who did not use these positive skills not only exhibited more negative behaviors but also reported fighting more often than the children who solved their problems in a positive way.[7]

As a general rule of thumb, I have found that problem-solving steps can be taught to children as young as seven years old. For children younger than this or for any child who has difficulty understanding the problem-solving steps, put your energy into teaching them the communication and sibling survival skills that I discuss in Steps Five and Seven. Move on to problem solving only when they can fully understand and participate in the problem-solving process.

As I pointed out in Step Five, one of the benefits of teaching your children how to work through problems effectively is that you get them focused on finding a solution instead of just arguing and complaining about the problem. Second, as you practice problem-solving skills together, you have a chance to show your children firsthand how to solve problems by working together in a way that pleases God and builds family relationships. Finally, as the research has demonstrated, teaching children how to work through problems respectfully and cooperatively is an extremely effective way of reducing sibling conflict. Let's now take a look at how you can add this important seed to your family soil.

ESTABLISHING GROUND RULES

One of the reasons that problem solving is effective in reducing sibling conflict is that there are certain ground rules that are established to make the problem-solving experience positive and productive. With practice, your children will eventually become more skilled in solving sibling problems on their own in a respectful and effective way. But the first step is to teach them the ground rules that make it all possible.

Robert and his family had not gone over these ground rules during their first problem-solving attempt. As a result, Robert proceeded to violate most of them in short order. His parents' mistakes didn't help any either.

"That's a stupid idea," Robert spat out in response to a suggestion offered by his brother.

"Hey, knock it off," Mr. Williams replied, annoyed that his son was already dragging the process down the tubes.

"I don't want to do this, the whole thing is dumb," Robert continued. "You say an idea, then you say an idea, and everything will all work out and we'll all get along. What kind of stupid idea is that?"

"I knew this would happen," Mrs. Williams sighed in frustration. "I just knew he'd wreck everything."

"Yeah, that's right, Mom. I wreck everything. While little angel-boy over there doesn't do anything wrong. Isn't that right?" Robert shouted.

When you begin the problem-solving process, you will see your children's old bad habits immediately emerge. You may see some of your own as well. This is what happened in Robert's family. Robert criticized his brother's positive attempts and then tried to sabotage the whole family meeting. Mr. Williams was unable to effectively redirect Robert, and Mrs. Williams reinforced his role as the family troublemaker. That was all Robert needed to spiral out of control.

These old habits are part of the problem and are one of the main reasons problems don't get worked out. The key to effective problem solving is doing things a new way, and in the process, helping your children develop new habits. Here are five ground rules that will make your problem-solving efforts a positive and productive experience.

1. No criticizing, name-calling, or put-downs allowed.

For problem-solving to be effective, the communication must be respectful. Your children are free to voice their opinions and feelings, as long as they do it respectfully. The insistence on respectful communication is a large part of what makes problem solving different from a typical sibling argument. No communication hazards allowed here.

2. Respect each other's views.

Problem solving never demands that your children agree with each other. However, they must be respectful of each other's views. There is a big difference between disagreeing on an issue and being disrespectful in how you communicate your differing views. Each family member has the right to his or her own opinion and will be expected to respect the right of others to have their opinions as well.

3. Take turns talking.

It is important for each person involved in the problem-solving process to have a chance to share his or her views. Make sure that one person does not dominate the discussion or take it over. As for your part, do not succumb to the temptation to lecture your children during this time. Everyone must get a chance to talk, which means that everyone else will need to listen.

4. Be brief and to the point.

You want to make the problem-solving process fun and productive for everybody. This is done by setting a quick and lively pace as you work through the problem-solving steps. Encourage everyone to keep their comments brief and to the point. If someone strays off topic, or gets bogged down on a tangential issue, politely steer them back on course.

5. Three "zaps" and you're out for five minutes.

In their book *Parents and Adolescents Living Together*, researchers Marion Forgatch and Gerald Patterson suggest using "zaps" to squelch negative behavior during the problem-solving process. Choose one person to be the mediator of your problem-solving discussion. You can take turns with a different person being the mediator for each discussion. The mediator is to watch carefully for ground-rule violations, and when he or she sees one, simply say, "Zap." When a person receives three zaps, the person earns the consequence of leaving the discussion for five minutes. This consequence applies equally to parents and children alike.

You might be asking yourself, "What if the person *wants* to leave the discussion?" In my experience, this seldom happens when the rest of the problem-solving process is followed. When a problem-solving discussion allows everyone to share their views and moves along at a quick and lively pace, most children and teens want to stay and be involved. They realize that decisions are going to be made that will affect them whether they are there or not, and they don't want to give up their ability to have input into the outcome of the discussion.

When Robert was breaking the ground rules during their problem-solving discussion, Mr. Williams could have simply said, "Robert, that's a zap." Robert might have replied, "So what?" Mr. Williams would have said, "Two more and you'll be out of the discussion for five minutes. Now, let's get back on topic. Where were we?" If Robert wanted to, he could continue to misbehave until he earned three zaps and was asked to leave. Then the discussion would go on without him and decisions would be made without Robert's input. If Robert didn't like the decisions, he would have to live with them until the next problem-solving discussion. Chances are that he would be more involved the next time around.

GROUND RULES

1. No criticizing, name-calling, or put-downs allowed.
2. Respect each other's views.
3. Take turns talking.
4. Be brief and to the point.
5. Three "zaps" and you're out for five minutes.

The first step of the problem-solving process is to review the ground rules. I suggest you print them on a piece of paper and hand them out to everyone. Explain and discuss each ground rule until everyone understands them. Choose the person who will be the mediator for the discussion and then move to the problem-solving steps.

TEACHING THE S.T.E.P.S.

Speaking of the workplace, Judith Bardwick stated, "Nothing creates more self-respect among employees than being included in the process of making decisions." This is exactly what you are about to do with your children as you work through important sibling problems. You are going to give them the privilege of being involved in family problem solving. These five problem-solving steps can be used to effectively tackle any sibling or family problem. Here are the five problem-solving steps with a brief description and example of each.

1. **S**tate the problem.
2. **T**hink of solutions.
3. **E**valuate the solutions.
4. **P**ick a solution.
5. **S**ee if it worked.

1. State the problem.

As Charles Kettering said, "A problem well-stated is a problem half-solved." The goal of the first step is to give everyone a chance to state the problem from his or her perspective. This is a great chance to use the communication skills you learned in Step Five. The sentence, "When _____ *(name the behavior you don't like)*, then _____ *(say how it is a problem for you)*" is a perfect way to help your children state the problem in a productive way.

Avoid identifying another person or a characteristic of that person as the problem. For instance, the statement "The problem is that James is a stupid jerk" is not a particularly helpful way for Sally to state the problem. That sentence would earn Sally a zap and she could try again to identify the behavior or situation that is a problem for her. A better way for Sally to state the problem would be, "When James makes faces at me during dinner, I don't like it and I feel really mad." Go around your family circle, allowing each person to state the problem from their perspective in a respectful way.

Example:

Dad: "Okay, now that everyone understands the ground rules, let's start solving our first problem. Let's talk about the fighting that has been going on when you guys are watching TV together."

Mom: "Yes, that's a good one. Now, the first step is to state the problem. Kayla, why don't you start, and since this is our first time, let's use this sentence to help us:
'When _____ *(state the behavior you don't like)*, then _____ *(say how it is a problem for you)*.'"

Kayla: "All right. Mitch, when you change the channels when I'm watching a show, I think that's really rude and I wish you would stop."

Mitchell: "Well, if you wouldn't watch such stupid shows—"

Dad: "That's a zap, Mitch."

Mitchell: "Awwww."

Kayla: "I think I'm going to like this."

Mom: "Now, Mitchell, why don't you state the problem from your point of view . . . respectfully please."

2. Think of solutions.

Here's where you need a pad of paper and a pencil. Your goal is to help your children make a creative list of possible solutions. In this type of brainstorming, virtually any suggestion goes (don't worry, you'll evaluate them later). By aiming for between five to ten solutions, you will help your children develop the habit of moving beyond the first one or two solutions that pop into their minds and learn to creatively think of new ways to solve the problem. You will be amazed at the solutions they can come up with.

Begin this step by saying, "Now we're going to make a list of possible solutions for this problem. Let's go around the circle and take turns saying our solutions, one at a time." Allow each person to say one solution, then move to the next person. Go around the family circle several times, until everyone has had a chance to suggest several possible solutions. Solutions can include ways to prevent the problem, guidelines for certain situations, ideas for making tasks more enjoyable, rewards for positive behavior, and negative consequences for disrespectful behavior.

Example:

Mom: "How about if we go to the next step, if everyone is ready. Let's take turns suggesting possible solutions for this problem. I'll write them down. Who would like to go first?"

Mitchell: "I will. How about Kayla doesn't watch TV."

Mom: "Okay, got it."

Kayla: "Very funny. How about if Mitchell doesn't watch TV."

Mom: "Got that one too."

Dad: "How about if there is no TV for either of you for one week the next time there is a disrespectful argument over channels?"

Mom: "Ooooh, that's a good one. I've got one, how about if we put stricter limits on the amount of time either of you watch TV. For example, no TV until all of your homework is done."

Mitchell: "How about if we take turns picking shows. Kayla chooses the shows one day and I choose the next."

Mom: "Okay, very creative."

3. Evaluate the solutions.

Once you have your list of solutions, the next step is to evaluate them together. The solutions that are ultimately chosen need to work for everyone. This can be seen in the story of the young boy who was having difficulty sharing with his brother one winter. "Honey," scolded his mother, "you shouldn't always keep everything for yourself. I've told you over and over again that you should let your brother play with your toys half of the time." "I've been doing it," the boy said. "I take the sled going downhill and he takes it going up."

Going around your family circle, have each person rate each solution by giving the solutions either a plus (+) or a minus (-) rating, depending on how well they think the solution would solve the problem. Record the ratings for each solution. You can ask your children to explain their evaluations ("Why did you give that solution a plus?") anytime you like.

Example:

Dad: "We have a lot of solutions now; why don't we evaluate them? The first one is no TV for Kayla. Mitchell, your rating?"

Mitchell: "A definite plus."

Mom: "Okay, Kayla?"

Kayla: "Minus."

Dad: "I'll give that one a minus too."

Mom: "So will I. Okay, the next solution is . . . no TV for Mitchell. Mitchell, your rating?"

Mitchell: "Minus."

Kayla: "Hmmmm, let me think . . . PLUS!"

Dad: "Minus for me."

Mom: "Me too. All right, the next solution is no TV for both of you for one week the next time there is an argument over channels."

Mitchell: "Minus for sure."

Kayla: "Minus."

Dad: "Kayla, why do you give that one a minus?"

Kayla: "I just think it's kind of harsh . . . a whole week?"

Dad: "I see what you mean, but I still like it, so I'll give it a plus. Maybe we can revise it later."

Mom: "Sounds good, I'll give it a plus too."

4. Pick a solution.

Once you have rated all of the solutions and have discussed the ratings as much as you want, it is time to narrow down to the top solutions.

PROBLEM-SOLVING SHEET

Problem: Fighting over the TV

Solutions:	Mitch	Kayla	Dad	Mom
1. No TV for Kayla.	+	–	–	–
2. No TV for Mitchell.	–	+	–	–
3. No TV for both for one week following fighting over TV.	–	–	+	+
4. No TV until homework done.	–	+	+	+
5. Take turns choosing channels each day.	+	+	+	–
6. Alternate choosing shows each hour.	–	+	+	+
7. Any fighting over TV means TV immediately goes off.	+	–	+	+
8. Each day with no TV fighting earns one point. Ten points earns each child a special privilege.	+	+	+	+
9. No TV for two days for both kids following fighting over the TV.	–	–	+	+
10. Take disputes to parents if cannot resolve on own.	+	+	+	+

(Column header for Mitch–Mom group: "Evaluations")

Put a star by the solutions that have the most pluses and read this list out loud. This is your new "short list." You can add new solutions to the mix and evaluate them, even during this stage of the discussion. In fact, you will find that your discussion will often prompt new ideas as you go.

After you have read the best solutions out loud, identify which one solution, or combination of solutions, would best solve the problem. Keep in mind that any solution or solutions that are chosen must ultimately be approved by the parents. Discuss the specific details of how you would put these solutions to work. You are now formalizing a plan for solving the problem. When you have a plan worked out, write it down in detail for later reference.

Example:

> Mom: "Okay, guys, the solutions with three or four pluses are . . ." *(Mom reads the list.)*
>
> Dad: "That's quite a few. We did pretty good. Okay, which ones do you guys think would solve the problem the best?"
>
> Kayla: "Probably taking turns choosing channels each hour, getting help if there's an argument, and getting points for no fighting."
>
> Mom: "Okay, but what should we do if there is an argument?"
>
> Dad: "I vote that the TV goes right off for the rest of the day, or for two days."
>
> Mom: "What do you guys think? We have to do something. Remember, it is not okay to be disrespectful or hurtful to each other when you're watching TV."
>
> Kayla: "But what if one person is trying to be respectful? Should they lose TV just because the other person is being rude?"
>
> Mom: "Great question, let's think about that."
>
> Dad: "How about if Mom or I decide who we think was trying to be respectful, and if we think you handled the situation right, you won't lose TV. The only person who will lose TV is the person your mom or I think acted disrespectfully, whether that is one or both of you."
>
> Mitchell: "I'm okay with that."
>
> Kayla: "That seems fair."

5. See if it worked.

Once you decide upon your plan, you need to give it a trial run. Decide how long you want to try your plan and then schedule a meeting to evaluate how things are going. You should wait no longer than one week before evaluating the effectiveness of your plan.

When you evaluate your plan, perhaps during your next family time, you may find that it is working well. If so, identify what everyone is doing to make things work so well, review the positive outcome that your plan is producing, and congratulate everyone on a job well done!

If your plan is not working well, identify where things are going wrong and go back to Step #2 to think of additional solutions. There may be a detail you forgot to work through or a circumstance that you failed to consider that is causing your plan to fail. After thinking of additional solutions, go through the rest of the steps for each new solution and adjust your plan as needed. If you run out of ideas for solutions, agree to do some family research, having everyone use their resources (e.g., friends, family members, books, pastors, teachers, counselors) to get new ideas for how to solve this problem. If you stay faithful to the problem-solving process, you should be able to find a good set of solutions for any sibling or family problem you run into.

Example:

> Dad: "Okay, everyone, we've tried our TV plan for one week. How do you think it's working?"
>
> Mom: "I think there's been less fighting over the TV."
>
> Mitchell: "I think I got robbed when you wouldn't let me watch TV on Friday."
>
> Mom: "Well, you were disrespectful, as I recall."
>
> Mitchell: "Yeah, you just didn't hear her."
>
> Kayla: "I was not disrespectful; you're the one who kicked the remote control."
>
> Mom: "Mitchell, if you lost TV privileges, it wasn't because of what Kayla did. It was because of how you chose to handle things. Right?"
>
> Mitchell: "Yeah, but what about her?"

Dad: "Guys, Mom and I are not psychic. We'll be as fair as we can in determining who we think is being respectful and who is not. That makes it your job to be so respectful that there's less chance we'll make a mistake. If either of you tries to be sneaky, sooner or later you'll get caught and you'll learn that being sneaky wasn't a very good idea."

Mom: "Let's focus on how we can keep our plan working well. Does anyone have any suggestions for improving the plan?"

Mitchell: "Naw, it's fine. Hey, how many points do I have?"

Dad: "I think you have five. Kayla, you have six."

Mom: "Hey, both of you are getting close to your special privilege. Good job!"

SAMPLE SOLUTIONS FOR THREE COMMON SIBLING PROBLEMS

There are many different sibling problems that you will tackle with your problem-solving steps. As you and your children gain more experience with this process, you will find that thinking of creative solutions becomes easier. To help you get started, here are sample solutions for three common sibling problems. Use any of these ideas in combination with your own. Notice the different ideas for preventing the problems, using creative guidelines and time limits, inserting positive and negative consequences, and emphasizing responsibility and respect.

Taking Turns with Computer/Video Games

If your children have trouble sharing the computer for games, here are some possible solutions:

1. Can only use electronics with parents' permission.
2. Can play no longer than thirty minutes by self if other person is waiting.
3. Use timer if parents ask you to.
4. Play two-player games when possible to include everyone.
5. If there is a disagreement about how to handle it, ask Mom or Dad.

6. Whoever is disrespectful will immediately lose all electronics for the day.
7. Extra playing time may be given if parents observe cooperative behavior and encouraging comments.

Name-Calling and Teasing

If your children have trouble with calling each other names and teasing each other, here are some possible solutions:

1. All name-calling and teasing off-limits.
2. If you get mad, use "When . . ." sentence instead of name-calling or teasing.
3. Respectfully ask person to stop name-calling or teasing.
4. Ignore and walk away.
5. If person doesn't stop, get parents.
6. If person continues teasing over time, let parents know.
7. Each day with no name-calling or teasing earns one point. Fifteen points earns special privilege.
8. Immediate time-out and thirty minutes of early bed for anyone who name-calls or teases.

Using Personal Possessions without Asking

If your children have trouble with "borrowing" each other's possessions without asking, here are some possible solutions:

1. Each have spot in room for private items. Cannot go in other's private spot.
2. Let parents and siblings know if you want siblings to ask before using a special item. Parents will give okay if reasonable.
3. All other items can be used if you are not available to ask.
4. Treat other's belongings respectfully.
5. If you damage something, you may have to pay for it. Parents will decide.
6. Using other's special belongings without permission earns immediate negative consequence. Parents will decide what the consequence will be.

QUESTIONS FOR REFLECTION

1. How skilled are you at using problem-solving steps in your own life?

2. Which ground rules will you have to emphasize the most with your children?

3. What sibling or family problems can you address using problem-solving steps? Which problems might be the easiest to begin with?

4. If you have never used these problem-solving steps before, what will be the hardest part about using them with your children? How can you overcome that obstacle?

5. Read Ephesians 6:4 and Proverbs 22:6. How does teaching your children to effectively solve problems play a role in obeying these verses?

6. What do you think your children will learn by working through sibling problems with the problem-solving steps?

PRAYER SUGGESTIONS

As you close this time, ask God to give you patience as you teach your children how to work through problems together. Pray that God will use these problem-solving steps to help your family learn to talk through difficult issues in a respectful way that honors him. Ask him to continue to shape you into the leader and example that your children need you to be.

PRACTICE MAKES PERFECT

1. How would you respond to this comment, made during a problem-solving discussion: "You have the stupidest ideas."

2. Make a list of possible solutions for Steven and Jenny (both teenagers) having problems sharing the bathroom in the morning before school. *(You will find sample responses on page 231.)*

For your next family time, use Family Discussion Guide #9: Let's Solve This Problem.

STEP SEVEN

TEACH SIBLING SURVIVAL SKILLS

In the year 1911, the historic race began for who would be the first person to reach the South Pole. Leading the two courageous teams were Norwegian explorer Roald Amundsen and British naval officer Robert Falcon Scott.

Amundsen's approach was one of exquisite planning, considering every facet of the trip in painstaking detail. After much research and consideration, Amundsen had skis specially made for the trip and imported dogs that would pull their supply sleds. He placed well-stocked supply depots along the route in strategic spots so that his men would not have to carry unnecessary supplies. He tested their equipment and made continual adjustments prior to beginning their expedition. Amundsen charted out the most direct route and anticipated every possible scenario. All of Amundsen's detailed planning paid off. Their team made the trip successfully in ninety-nine days and experienced virtually no significant setbacks.

Historians tell us that Scott's approach was characterized by a lack of planning, the antithesis of Amundsen's style. He unwisely chose to use motorized sledges and ponies as their primary mode of transportation. Unfortunately, the sledges froze and the ponies died in the extreme weather. As a result, the crew had to haul their own equipment. At the last minute, Scott decided to bring along an extra person, but did not supply additional provisions. This led to a shortage of food, water, and valuable equipment. Over time, Scott's crew experienced frostbite, snow blindness, and dehydration. While they eventually arrived at the South Pole, they found that Amundsen's team had beaten them by more than a month. Tragically, the trip had taken too much out of Scott's team and, despite their valiant efforts, they were found frozen to death in their tents eight months later.

FIVE SIBLING SURVIVAL SKILLS

As parents, too many of us approach the challenge of raising siblings like Scott rather than like Amundsen. We respond to sibling problems only after they have happened and spend too little time planning ahead to prevent potential problems.

One way to improve our children's sibling relationships is to identify the nature of their most common challenges and teach them how to handle those situations more effectively. As James 1:19–20 reminds us, "Everyone should be quick to listen, slow to speak and slow to become angry, for man's anger does not bring about the righteous life that God desires." One research study found that when older siblings behaved positively and cooperatively toward their younger siblings, the younger siblings demonstrated more mature behavior. Furthermore, friendly behavior by the younger siblings was related to an increase in positive behavior in the older siblings. In other words, positive behavior by one sibling seemed to increase the positive behavior of the other.[1]

In order to increase positive behavior when engaged in typical "everyday" sibling squabbles, there are five specific survival skills that every sibling needs to master:

1. Responding to sibling aggravation
2. Sharing
3. Taking turns
4. Being flexible
5. Forgiving each other

It would be nice if our children came equipped with these skills, but as we all know, they don't. Just telling them to improve doesn't do much good; we've got to teach them. Hall of Fame quarterback Roger Staubach said, "In business or in football, it takes a lot of unspectacular preparation to produce spectacular results." The same is true of parenting. You will have to invest some unspectacular time teaching your children these valuable survival skills, but when you do, the results can be more than spectacular.

Matthew and Calvin were taking turns playing a computer game together, with one watching while the other played, and vice versa. The boys usually took turns quite well on the computer, but this time things didn't go as usual.

"Stop it," shouted Matthew with an irritated tone, as he tried to concentrate on his game.

Greg, the boys' father, looked up from where he was reading on the couch just in time to see Matthew take two swings at Calvin, who was seated directly behind him.

"I said stop it!" Matthew growled.

Greg was not sure what the problem was until he saw Calvin quickly reach over and tap Matthew on the shoulder and then withdraw his hand just as quickly.

"I said stop it!" Matthew shouted again, his frustration rapidly growing.

Greg finally understood what was happening. While Matthew was trying to play his game, Calvin had been tapping him on the shoulder and then quickly moving his hand away. Matthew had asked him to stop, but Calvin had not been able to resist the temptation of continuing his aggravating fun. After asking him to stop again, Matthew had taken a couple of frustrated swings in an effort to stop his sibling tormentor.

Matthew needed to learn the very difficult skill of responding to sibling aggravation (without getting himself into trouble). At other times, he and his brother both needed to be able to share, take turns, show flexibility, and forgive each other for things they say and do. The best lectures are not enough to teach these skills. Children must practice thinking, saying, and doing the right things in order to be able to demonstrate these five survival skills in real life.

DEVELOP A THINK/SAY/DO PLAN

Each of these skills can be broken down into what I call a "think/say/do plan." While the "say" and "do" components may seem obvious, you may not have considered the "think" component before. It is crucial that your children think the right things, because it is their unseen, automatic thoughts that set the course for the words and actions that follow. Negative, angry, or shortsighted thoughts pave the way for negative words and actions. You want your children's thoughts to be balanced, accurate, and reflective of biblical teaching. When their thinking is on track, it is easier for their words and actions to stay on track as well.

Thinking, saying, and doing the right things are essential for truly mastering each skill. For children younger than seven, however, it may be necessary to begin with only the "say and do" part of the plan, as discussing and memorizing thoughts may be too abstract and difficult for them. This is fine; just save the thinking component for when they are older and can conceptualize their thoughts more easily. For these children, you will develop a "say and do" plan.

Before you read the think/say/do plans for these five sibling survival skills, let me give you a little glimpse at some of the think/say/do plans your children may be using now.

Situation #1:

Ashley is quietly reading a book in the family room when her younger brother, Kendall, walks in, plops down on the couch with a comic book, and starts loudly drumming on his legs.

Think: Ashley's attention is immediately interrupted and she thinks, *He knows I'm reading; how can he be so inconsiderate! He's always trying to wreck everything I do. I can never get a quiet moment around here!*

Say: Feeling annoyed, Ashley says to Kendall in an irritated voice, "Do you mind? I happen to be reading over here. Or are you too blind to notice that?"

Do: Kendall responds with a smirk and begins drumming even louder on his legs. Ashley jumps to her feet, grabs the comic book out of Kendall's hand, and throws it into the kitchen. Then she stomps to her room, slamming the door behind her.

Situation #2:

Jonathan is playing with several toys in the playroom. Joel walks over and asks if he can use one of the toys Jonathan is playing with.

Think: Immediately Jonathan thinks, *Joel is always bugging me! I wish he'd just leave me alone.*

Say: Jonathan looks up at Joel and says with a taunting smile, "You can't use them because I'm using them."

Do: Jonathan then immediately gathers up all of the toys, even a few that he wasn't using, and forms them into a big pile in front of himself so that he can guard them. Joel starts crying and runs off to tell Mom.

Your children are always using think/say/do plans, but as you can see, they often use the wrong ones! These negative think/say/do plans are guaranteed to fuel sibling resentment and spiral sibling conflicts out of control until your children end up getting sent to separate time-out spots. In order to stop the negative think/say/do plans that your children are currently using, you need to teach them think/say/do plans that will really work.

Here are think/say/do plans for each of the five sibling survival skills. Read them through, and then I'll show you how to teach them to your children.

1. Responding to sibling aggravation

Think: (choose one or two)

> *Maybe he doesn't know this is bothering me.*
> *Just because he's going to get into trouble doesn't mean I have to.*
> *I'm going to handle this the right way.*
> *This is frustrating, but God will help me do the right thing.*

Say: (in a firm, but respectful way)

"When you _____, then _____." (Say how you feel or how the behavior causes a problem for you.)

"Please stop _____." (Say the behavior that is bothering you.)

"Would you please stop _____." (Say it more strongly the second time.)

"If you don't stop, I'll get Mom/Dad."

Do:

> Ignore.
> Go somewhere else.
> Walk away and do something else.
> Go and get help from your parents.

2. Sharing

Think: (choose one or two)

> *Everyone has to share sometimes.*
> *God wants me to treat others the way I want them to treat me.*
> *If I share with _____, she'll probably share with me.*
> *Sharing is a good way to have fun together.*

Say: (in a friendly way)

> "I'm using it now, but you can use it later."
> "Sure you can use it." (Then find something else you can use.)
> "Maybe we can play with this together."
> "Maybe you can use _____." (Suggest something else she can use.)

Do:

> Share the toy and/or continue to play in a friendly way.

3. Taking turns

Think: (choose one or two)

> *It doesn't just belong to me.*
> *Taking turns is considerate, and that makes God happy.*
> *If I don't take turns, then I won't be able to play.*
> *It's his turn now; I'll go again when it's my turn.*

Say: (in a friendly way)

> "Okay, it's your turn."
> "You can go now."

Do:

> Give ball/dice/controls/game piece to person in a friendly way.

4. Being flexible

Think: (choose one or two)

I can't always get my way.

I can have fun doing what he wants this time.

Maybe I can do it my way some other time.

It would be friendly to let _____ do it her way this time.

Say: (in a respectful way)

"Okay, that will be fun."

"Okay, we can do it your way this time."

"That's okay, I don't mind."

"Maybe we can do what I want some other time."

Do:

Do the activity in a friendly way.

Find something else to do.

Wait your turn.

5. Forgiving each other

Think: (choose one or two)

I do some things that I shouldn't do too.

God wants me to forgive him.

Everyone makes mistakes.

Sometime, I'll probably have to ask her to forgive me too.

Say: (in a respectful way)

"That's okay."

"I didn't like that very much, but I forgive you."

"We all make mistakes, so I forgive you."

Do:

Go on with normal activities.

The idea is simple. First you think the right thing. Then you say the right thing. Then you do the right thing. These think/say/do plans are far superior to what we saw Ashley and Jonathan do in Situations #1 and

#2. Each thought, word, and action is respectful and balanced. Like dominoes, each component leads to the other, helping your children to handle difficult sibling situations respectfully and without getting into trouble. And, most important, each think/say/do plan can be taught and learned.

TEACHING SIBLING SURVIVAL SKILLS

A study conducted by the U.S. Department of Health, Education, and Welfare found that learners retain ten percent of what they read, twenty percent of what they hear, fifty percent of what they see and hear, but *ninety* percent of what they *say* and *do*. As the Chinese proverb reminds us, "I hear and I forget. I see and remember. I do and I understand."

You can teach your children these valuable survival skills in your family times by using the five Family Time Discussion Guides at the end of the book that correspond with this chapter. I remember when Lora and I taught our boys a think/say/do plan for sharing a few years ago. We went through each of the steps and had a fun time rehearsing the skill in our family times. When I would come home from work, the boys would often ask me, "Dad, can we practice now?" and we would do a quick practice.

During the next few months, Lora and I would occasionally happen upon a "sharing" situation unfolding before our eyes. For instance, Jacob

FOR A LAUGH

Sibling Survival Skills You DON'T Want Your Children to Learn

1. Embarrassing things to do with your sister's training bra
2. How to tattle like a pro
3. 101 uses for naked baby pictures
4. The art of faking an injury ("He hit me . . .")
5. How to look innocent when everyone knows you did it
6. How to name-call without moving your lips
7. 101 creative ways to use itching powder

would be playing with some cars and Luke wanted to use one of the cars that Jacob was using. Immediately, before things had a chance to go wrong, we would remind Jacob to use his plan. Since we had practiced regularly, he knew just what we were talking about and you could see the light bulb go on inside his head. He knew exactly what to do. This was his chance to show us he could do it.

"I'm using this car right now, but you can use it later," Jacob said. "Why don't you use this one, Luke? It goes fast."

Just like we had practiced! His eyes immediately turned to us for approval.

"Excellent job using your plan, pal!" we responded with enthusiasm. "That was very respectful. And, Luke, that's a great way of waiting for your turn to use the car and finding a different car to use instead. This is a great car! You both are doing a great job of sharing and playing together!"

We pointed out how their sharing plan was helping them to have fun and talked about what would have happened if one or both of them had not been acting respectfully.

"Remember, boys, you guys could have ended up in time-out if you had treated each other disrespectfully, and that would have been very sad," I said. "But look at you guys, both still having fun because you're sharing and taking turns."

In the same way, you will have real-life opportunities to remind your children to use the skills that you have taught and practiced together. The more you discuss and rehearse them, the easier it will be for your children to use them. The more bonded together you are as a family and the richer your family soil, the more they will *want* to use them.

These skills will take time to master and there will certainly be occasions when your kids will abandon them altogether. There were many times when one or both of our children lost privileges and/or were sent to time-out because they failed to use their plans, and this still happens today. But that is a natural part of the learning process. With time and practice, you will see your children's ability to use these valuable survival skills improve. And when you have created a healthy family soil and planted the right seeds, you will see their sibling relationships improve right along with them.

QUESTIONS FOR REFLECTION

1. Do your children need to learn the five sibling survival skills? Why?

2. Of the five sibling survival skills, which do your children struggle with the most?

3. Read Proverbs 6:6–8 and 22:6. What do you think about the idea of teaching your children survival skills to prepare them to handle difficult relational challenges? Do you think that is part of the training God wants you to do with your children?

4. Why is the "think" part of the think/say/do plan so important?

5. Will your children learn these skills if you just lecture them, or do they need to practice them together? Why?

6. I have suggested beginning with the survival skill of Responding to Sibling Aggravation. Feel free to begin with a different survival skill if you would like to. When you have chosen your skill, review the Family Time Discussion Guide for that skill at the end of the book. Be prepared with situations to role-play for your family time rehearsals—and have fun.

PRAYER SUGGESTIONS

Close this time with prayer, thanking God for blessing you with each of your children. Ask him to give you patience and guidance and to make you the teacher your children need as you show them these important sibling survival skills. Commit your family times to God and ask that he will continue to use them to shape each of your children's hearts and lives.

PRACTICE MAKES PERFECT

To practice thinking of creative options for think/say/do plans, identify one additional thing your children can think, say, and do for each of the five survival skills.

Responding to sibling aggravation:

Think: _____

Say: _____

Do: _____

Sharing:

Think: _____

Say: _____

Do: _____

Taking turns:

Think: _____

Say: _____

Do: _____

Being flexible:

Think: _____

Say: _____

Do: _____

Forgiving each other:

Think: _____

Say: _____

Do: _____

(You will find sample responses on page 231.)

For your next family time, use Family Time Discussion Guide #10: Responding to Sibling Aggravation.

PROVIDE THE RIGHT
ENVIRONMENT

REINFORCE POSITIVE SIBLING BEHAVIOR

Ten-year-old Phillip was sitting on the couch in my office, fiddling with one of the small trinkets I have for just that purpose. We were talking about what he liked to do, how he liked school, and who his friends were. Phillip spoke easily and was refreshingly candid as he described these different areas of his life.

The discussion moved to his family relationships. After getting the names and ages of his siblings, we explored how they all got along.

"So, how do you guys get along with each other?" I asked.

"We fight all the time," Phillip said with a smile.

I wasn't sure what bothered me more, the statement that Phillip and his siblings fought constantly, or the fact that Phillip seemed pleased about it.

"Can you tell me what you mean?" I inquired.

"My sister is always bugging me and I always get her back!" Phillip said with a triumphant grin.

"What do you mean, you always get her back?" I probed, afraid of what I was going to hear next.

"REVENGE!" Phillip said in a drawn-out voice, rubbing his hands together with a sinister grin on his face and an excited twinkle in his eyes.

Phillip went on to explain the endless game of "You bugged me so now I'm going to bug you back" that he and his sister Katrina were continuously engaged in. He seemed oblivious about his role in maintaining this state of tension with Katrina and felt entirely justified in his negative actions toward her. After all, he could recite a laundry list of negative behaviors that she had done to him.

As we talked, I couldn't help but think that part of Phillip actually enjoyed the challenge of seeing who would win. Who would come out on top. Who could annoy, aggravate, and torment the other the worst. And, most important, who could be sly enough to get away with it.

It was obvious that Phillip's negative behavior toward Katrina was paying off. Phillip was clearly overjoyed when his attempts at getting even were successful. The challenge of trying to enact revenge upon his sibling nemesis without getting detected by his parents was more exhilarating than a video game and was all the reward he needed.

WHERE IS THE PAYOFF?

One of the questions you need to ask yourself about negative sibling behavior is, "How is this behavior paying off?" Children do not purposely do things they think will work out badly. They do things they think will work out well for them, in either the short term or the long term. Sometimes the potential payoff is obvious, while other times it is subtle or almost impossible to figure out. But make no mistake, when a child repeats a behavior, he or she is expecting it to accomplish something.

For example, when Charles stealthily punches Abram on the leg in the backseat of the car, he is expecting some sort of payoff. Maybe the payoff is revenge for when Abram tattled on him yesterday. Perhaps it is the overdramatic reaction Abram is sure to give to his parents. It may be the challenge of seeing if he can get away with it. The *immediate* payoff for a negative behavior is often strong enough to entice a child to commit the behavior even though there is a chance that a negative consequence may result in the long term. Charles knew that a stern look from Mom was likely, but compared to the satisfaction of getting away with his sneak attack, he was willing to take his chances.

In order for a seed to blossom into a beautiful flower, it must have the right environment: an environment that promotes growth. Your job is to create a family environment that takes the payoff out of the wrong place and puts it in the right place. You create this environment by asking yourself a second important question: "What do I want my children to learn?"

WHAT DO YOU WANT THEM TO LEARN?

In terms of sibling relationships, you want your children to learn several important lessons:

1. Treating each other in a friendly way works out well.
2. Communicating angry feelings respectfully and taking the time to talk through problems are always worth the extra effort they require.
3. Sharing, taking turns, and letting someone else go first can be fun.
4. Being flexible when things don't go your way isn't so bad after all.
5. When someone else acts disrespectfully toward them, they don't have to respond in kind.
6. While it requires hard work and not always getting their way, obeying God's commands about how they should treat each other is always the best thing to do.

As James wrote, "But the man who looks intently into the perfect law that gives freedom, and continues to do this, not forgetting what he has heard, but doing it—he will be blessed in what he does" (James 1:25).

One study asked fourth- and fifth-grade children what their parents can do to most effectively decrease sibling fighting. The three interventions that were rated as the most effective by these children were getting a treat for being good, being disciplined, and being kept busy with fun activities.[1] It is telling that two of their three top responses included receiving positive and negative consequences based on how they treat their siblings.

Simply stated, there are only two types of behavior in sibling relationships: respectful and disrespectful. You want to create a family environment that will encourage your children to use the respectful living-together skills that you have been teaching them in your family times. When they consistently experience that using these skills and treating each other respectfully pays off, your children will be able to see for themselves how following God's commands brings endless benefits, while disobeying them brings only sadness.

INCREASING POSITIVE SIBLING BEHAVIOR

Brad's parents realized that they had not been providing very much positive attention for their son's respectful behavior. After we talked together about Brad's disrespectful behavior at home and with his younger brother, Mr. and Mrs. Miller decided to work on improving the way they paid attention when Brad made good choices.

Mrs. Miller started noticing when Brad let his younger brother sit in the best chair for watching TV. She hadn't realized that he had been doing that. She also became aware that Brad usually brushed his teeth without arguing and often was very friendly when playing action figures with his brother.

Mr. Miller took notice when he saw Brad listen to his mother without having to be asked twice. He also heard Brad say, "Nice try" when his brother missed a shot playing basketball in the driveway.

When Mr. and Mrs. Miller noticed these respectful behaviors, they began to let Brad know how much they appreciated them.

"Honey, I really liked the way you let Aaron use your baseball mitt just now."

"I sure like how you two guys are playing together so nicely and sharing so well. You're both doing great!"

"Hey, pal, that was great listening to Mom just now. When she asked you to put your shoes on, you got up and did it the first time she asked you. That was super!"

When I saw Mr. and Mrs. Miller a few weeks later in my office, they told me about the changes they had made. "I think he knows we're paying more attention to him," Mrs. Miller said.

"And I think he likes it," Mr. Miller added with a smile.

"Do you notice any change in his behavior?" I asked.

"I think we do," Mrs. Miller answered. "I mean, he's not perfect yet, don't get me wrong. But I think it is a bit better. And it helps me too, to realize that he actually is making a lot of good choices."

Though you may never have thought of it, increasing positive sibling behavior is an excellent way of reducing sibling conflict. The equation is simple: the more your children are playing respectfully and cooperatively, the less they are bickering and fighting. In fact, watching for and reinforcing positive sibling behavior has been proven to increase cooperative sibling behavior and reduce sibling fighting.[2] There are two different types of positive reinforcement that you can use to increase your children's positive sibling behavior. Here is a description of each.

Positive Attention

Everyone likes receiving positive attention. Who doesn't enjoy being told they have done a good job, feel warm following a reassuring squeeze on the shoulder, or appreciate being recognized for their hard work? In their best-selling book *The One Minute Manager*, Ken Blanchard and Spencer Johnson revolutionized the business management world by applying this simple truth to the workplace. Take a look at what they said about the impact that positive attention can have in a work environment when it is given the right way.

> The young man made a few notes in his notebook and then asked, "What happens, Mr. Levy, when the One Minute Manager catches you doing something right?"
>
> "That's when he gives you a One Minute Praising," Levy said with some delight.
>
> "What does that mean?" the young man wanted to know.
>
> "Well, when he has seen that you have done something right, he comes over and makes contact with you. That often includes putting his hand on your shoulder or briefly touching you in a friendly way."
>
> "Doesn't that bother you," the young man wondered, "when he touches you?"
>
> "No!" Levy insisted. "On the contrary, it helps. I know he really cares about me and he wants me to prosper.... When he makes contact, it's brief, but it lets me know once again that we're really on the same side."
>
> "Anyway, after that," Levy continued, "he looks you straight in the eye and tells you precisely what you did right. Then he shares with you how good he feels about what you did."
>
> "I don't think I've ever heard of a manager doing that," the young man broke in. "That must make you feel pretty good."
>
> "It certainly does," Levy confirmed.

Whether in the workplace, on the soccer field, or in your own family room, positive attention from the person in charge is a powerful motivator. For your children, the person in charge is you. In Steps One and Three, we talked about pointing out your children's positive behaviors, making regular physical contact, and giving frequent verbal affirmations as ways of giving attention to all of your children and building strong family relationships. Now we are emphasizing the fact that when done in the right way, these actions also reinforce your children's positive sibling behavior, teaching them that communicating respectfully and cooperating with each other bring positive results. As your children come to understand this, they will actually *want* to act this way more often. No kidding. As someone once said, "A person may not be as good as you tell her she is, but she'll try harder thereafter."

Desired Privileges

The second type of positive reinforcement that can be used to increase positive sibling behavior is the privileges that your children enjoy. Children have a myriad of positive activities that they like to engage in, including playing with certain toys, eating special snacks, watching television, listening to music, going to the zoo, talking on the phone, playing video games, going out to eat, watching movies, hosting sleep-overs, and so on. As you can see, these privileges include daily activities, special outings, or just about anything that is reinforcing to your child.

Before you get concerned that you are going to end up shamelessly bribing your children to get along, let me assure you that nothing is further from the truth. Your children *already* experience most of these desired activities on a regular or semiregular basis. You are simply going to be

FOR A LAUGH

How NOT to Use Positive Reinforcement

1. Tell your children you'll be their "friend for life" if they don't fight today.
2. Remind your children that because they didn't hit each other in the car, the big green swamp monster will let them live another day.
3. Toss peanut M&Ms to your children any moment that they are not touching each other.
4. Use a star chart to record days with no sibling fighting. Five stars earns a new Porsche.
5. Tell your children that for every day they get along, they get one day taken off school at the end of the year.

more purposeful about what they have to do to *earn* these desired privileges. That is not bribing, any more than it is bribery for you to receive a paycheck for completing your job duties. Instead, it is deciding ahead of time that respectful behavior is the only thing that will pay off.

Everyday privileges, such as TV, can easily be used to reinforce positive sibling behavior. These privileges can be used by both children if they use them in a cooperative and respectful way. If both children are respectful when watching TV together, for example, they earn the privilege of continuing to watch TV. If one child is acting disrespectfully while the other is *clearly* acting respectfully, then the child who acted disrespectfully must stop watching TV (and go to time-out) while the other child can continue to watch. If both children become disrespectful when watching TV, then they both lose the privilege. If you are not entirely sure who was disrespectful, then the TV can go off anyway. It is their job to be respectful if they want the TV to stay on. This rule can apply to any rewarding sibling activity your children participate in. The lesson they will learn is that respectful sibling behavior turns on fun activities while disrespectful sibling behavior turns them off.

Another simple way to increase positive sibling behavior is to have special privileges that are earned when your children get along for a certain amount of time. For instance, you can have an occasional special privilege, such as a pizza and movie night, that can be earned as the result of positive sibling behavior. Clearly define what kind of sibling behavior you are looking for (e.g., sharing, cooperating, talking respectfully) and what kind of behavior is off-limits (e.g., fighting, name-calling, shouting). Place an X on the calendar for each day of respectful sibling behavior. When your children earn five X's, a fun pizza and movie night can follow. Then, have your children choose another special privilege, set your goal for six X's, and do it again.

FOUR STEPS TO POSITIVE SIBLING BEHAVIOR

In order to use positive attention and desired privileges to increase your children's positive sibling behavior, there are four steps you must follow. These steps are simple to understand and absolutely essential if you want your children to learn that respectful sibling behavior really pays off.

1. Know your targets.

There is an old saying, "You can't hit a target if you don't have one." Make a list of the sibling behaviors that you would like your children to learn. These can include playing cooperatively, taking turns, letting the other person go first, talking respectfully, sitting in the backseat without fighting, expressing angry feelings respectfully, sharing toys and games, saying "thank you" and "please," making encouraging comments such as "good job," and so on.

Once you have your list of target behaviors, place them in rank order, with the behaviors you would like to increase first at the top of your list. The behaviors must be specific and observable, which means they must be things your children either say or do. "Liking each other" is not a good target, as it describes an inner attitude instead of a specific behavior you can observe. On the other hand, "playing cooperatively for ten minutes (without arguing or fighting)" is both specific and observable.

Once you have your list, focus on the top two behaviors. Let's say that your top two sibling behaviors for Johnny and Susie are: (1) sharing toys and (2) playing cooperatively for ten minutes. Both of these behaviors are specific and observable and make great targets. Now that you have your targets, let's work on how you can hit them.

2. Give immediate feedback.

In order to hit your targets, you must take careful aim. This means that you must be on the lookout for *every* instance your children display the target behaviors. In our example, this means any time Johnny or Susie share anything or play cooperatively for ten minutes (which means without arguing or fighting), you must be aware of it and immediately respond to it.

For most of us, this takes some practice. We are well trained at responding to our children's negative behavior, but most of us are not equally as good at looking for specific positive behaviors. But this is exactly what you must learn to do. This means that you must be on the lookout for the target behaviors *before* they happen. You must particularly be alert in situations where your target behaviors are likely to occur. For instance, anytime Johnny and Susie are playing a game together or are even playing in the same room, you need to be watching for any signs of sharing and keeping your eye on the clock to see if they approach ten minutes with no fighting.

Mary was a frustrated mother who was learning how to look for positive target behaviors in her two elementary-aged children. After she chose two target behaviors and I explained how she had to be on constant lookout for them, our session ended and Mary went home to practice her new skills.

One week later at our next session, I asked Mary, "Well, how are Jeremy and Teresa doing?"

"They've actually had a great week." Mary beamed. "There's still been some fighting, of course, but they got along better than usual."

"Do you think they actually got along better," I wondered out loud, "or did you just become more aware of their positive behavior?"

Mary understood my point and smiled. "I'm not sure," she replied, "maybe both."

Your goal is to be aware of *eighty to one hundred percent* of the time your children display the target sibling behaviors. Like Mary, most parents are surprised at how much positive behavior they have been overlooking. Once you observe your children's positive sibling behavior, you must immediately respond if you want to reinforce it effectively. But how do you respond in a way that will make your children want to do those behaviors again?

3. Describe the positive behavior and its outcome.

When your children display the target behaviors you are looking for, such as sharing, immediately walk over to them and gently touch them on the arm or shoulder. Describe the way they are talking or acting that you like and tell them how happy you are that they are doing this. Point out the benefits of their behavior, such as having fun, getting along with each other, helping your family, and so on.

You want your children to learn three things:

1. They are making positive choices about how to get along with each other.
2. You notice and appreciate these choices.
3. These choices bring definite benefits.

Here are some examples of how this might look and sound in action:

Situation: Allen and Terry have been playing cars together nicely for ten minutes.

Mom: *(walks over and places a hand on each child's shoulder)* "Hey, you guys, you're doing a great job at sharing and playing nicely together. No wonder you're having so much fun! I sure love watching you guys play."

Situation: Chloe offers to help Jennifer with her homework.

Dad: *(walks over and gently touches each girl on the arm)* "Chloe, I appreciate your trying to help Jen with homework. That's really being a great sister. And, Jen, I'm proud of you for working so hard on your homework and not giving up. That's how you get it done. You're really sticking with it."

Situation: Driving to the mall *(kids in the backseat).*

Mom: "I really like how everyone is getting along in the car right now. You're talking respectfully to each other and we're all having a fun time. No one's kicking each other or anything! You guys are each doing an excellent job. Tell you what, if you guys keep it up, maybe we can get a special snack at the mall. What do you think?"

Situation: Alec and Stuart are taking turns while playing a video game.

Dad: *(kneels down and touches each boy on the shoulder)* "I just wanted to tell you that you're both doing a great job taking turns and encouraging each other on this game right now. I've been watching you for the last few minutes, and I'm really proud of how you're doing. If you guys would have been arguing about your game, it would be off right now. But because you've been sharing and taking turns, we can put an X on our calendar. Two more X's and we can rent that video game you guys have been talking about. Keep up the good work!"

4. Be consistent.

The last essential step in teaching your children that positive sibling behavior pays off is to reinforce it consistently. Consider these two families:

1. Mark and Jim's parents remember to notice and comment on their positive sibling behavior about three times a month.
2. Debra and Ruth's parents notice and comment on their positive sibling behavior about ninety times a month (that's only three times a day!).

Over a span of three months, Debra and Ruth will have heard two hundred and sixty-one *more* positive comments about their sibling behavior than Mark and Jim. Which sibling pair do you think will show more positive sibling behavior?

As Goethe reminded us, "The way you see people is the way you treat them, and the way you treat them is what they become." If you want siblings who get along, then you have to start looking for that behavior. When you look for and immediately reinforce positive sibling behavior, you help your children to see it too. When they begin to see it and are reminded of the benefits it brings, they want to do it more often. The more often they do it, the stronger their skills become. The stronger their skills become, the easier it is to do. The easier it is to do, the more naturally they do it.

We all want to do things that pay off for us. Make sure your children learn that following God's command to "Do to others as you would have them do to you" (Luke 6:31) is always worth the effort it takes. In doing so, you will help them build positive relational habits that will benefit their sibling relationships and pay big dividends for your family.

FOUR STEPS TO POSITIVE SIBLING BEHAVIOR

1. Know your targets.
2. Give immediate feedback.
3. Describe the positive behavior and its outcome.
4. Be consistent.

QUESTIONS FOR REFLECTION

1. List five positive sibling behaviors that you would like to see your children display more often.

2. Read Jeremiah 32:19; Ephesians 6:8; and Hebrews 11:6. God makes it clear that he will reward those who obey him. How often do you point out or reinforce your children's positive sibling behavior?

3. How can you improve the effectiveness of the way you reinforce your children's positive sibling behavior?

4. Of the Four Steps to Positive Sibling Behavior, which do you need to improve the most?

5. List five desired privileges that you can logically link to positive sibling behavior.

6. Put together a simple plan for increasing one positive sibling behavior, using both positive attention and desired privileges.
   - Identify the behavior you want to increase.
   - Identify how you will use positive attention.
   - Identify how you will use desired privileges.

PRAYER SUGGESTIONS

Close this time in prayer, asking God to help you see your children as he sees them—to see the potential and purpose that he has placed in each one. Ask him to open your eyes to their positive behavior and to help you effectively reinforce their good choices. Determine to be a parent who helps your children learn that respectful sibling behavior is always the best choice.

PRACTICE MAKES PERFECT

1. How can you give your children positive attention when you observe them interacting in a friendly way as you walk through the mall?

2. How can you use desired privileges to reinforce your children making encouraging comments to each other?

   (You will find sample responses on page 232.)

For your next family time, choose from Family Time Discussion Guides #6–8 or #11–14.

USE SIBLING CONSEQUENCES THAT WORK

N ancy is the mother of three children, ages five, seven, and ten. As we talked in my office, she explained to me how her kids bickered and argued with each other and how this was hurting their family relationships. The latest development was that Nick, her oldest boy, was starting to hit his siblings when he became angry with them, which worried Nancy and her husband greatly.

We proceeded through the list of introductory questions I routinely ask parents when I meet them for the first time. Eventually, we reached the point where we discuss past and current attempts that parents have made to curb their children's negative behavior.

"What kinds of things have you guys tried in the past?" I inquired.

"Oh, the usual, I suppose," Nancy said.

"How about if you list the things you and Neil do when your children act negatively," I instructed, "placing them in order of which you do most often."

After a few seconds of honest thought, Nancy told me her most frequent response to negative sibling behavior. It just happened to be the same response that has been given by the majority of parents to whom I have asked this question.

"Well, after I tell them to stop and they just keep on doing it," Nancy began, "I guess I start shouting at them."

Is there anyone among us who has not shouted at our kids? Unfortunately, shouting is not only one of the most common responses that we all have made when faced with sibling conflict, it is also one of the most ineffective. While raising your volume a notch or two and still maintaining a sense of control and respect is perfectly acceptable, uncontrolled shouting and yelling misses the bar on several counts. Not only does shouting have minimal effect in reducing negative behavior over the long haul, it is prominent on our list of disrespectful communication hazards (see Step Five). Furthermore, when you shout at your children, you are giving them a model of the very behavior you *don't* want them to imitate.

When considering how to respond to negative sibling behavior, you need to ask yourself, "What do I want my children to learn about disrespectful behavior?" Here are four lessons I think you'll agree with:

1. Treating each other disrespectfully never pays off.
2. It never works out well to hurt someone with your words or actions.
3. Acting selfishly or inconsiderately never brings a good outcome.
4. Obeying God's commands about how to treat each other brings positive results and disobeying his commands brings negative results. Every time.

As Paul reminded the believers in Galatia, "Do not be deceived: God cannot be mocked. A man reaps what he sows. The one who sows to please his sinful nature, from that nature will reap destruction; the one who sows to please the Spirit, from the Spirit will reap eternal life" (Galatians 6:7–8).

DECREASING NEGATIVE SIBLING BEHAVIOR

When it comes to negative consequences, the first issue that parents have to decide upon is, "When do I intervene in a sibling conflict?" Some recommend a hands-off approach, supposing that children will learn to work it out if left to their own devices. However, as we discussed in Steps Five and Six, positive communication and problem-solving skills don't come naturally to most children. Thus, if children have not been taught these skills, there is no reason to think that they will magically work things out in a respectful way when left to resolve difficult conflicts on their own.

In fact, one author suggested that leaving siblings to "fight it out" on their own may actually result in one child regularly dominating over the other, away from the watchful eye of the parents. This negative domination can result in the weaker child feeling increasingly defeated and passively succumbing to the other sibling's tyranny out of a sense of "learned helplessness."[1]

Other sibling research found that when parents *intervened* in sibling conflict, the children's use of positive communication and problem-solving skills increased. The researchers reasoned that parental intervention gave the children a model of how to handle the conflict more appropriately and that children learned from observing how their parents handled the conflict. As a result of parental intervention, the intensity of the conflict was reduced and children's ability to effectively solve their problems improved.[2]

I recommend that you take a fluid approach to responding to sibling conflict. This means that once you have taught your children *how* to solve their problems effectively, you give them a chance to work things out. However, as soon as you are aware that they have reached their limit and that one or more of them is no longer handling the situation respectfully, you need to intervene. Occasionally, you might even intervene slightly before this point of no return, to help them stay on track and work it out in a productive way.

NEGATIVE CONSEQUENCES FOR SIBLINGS

There are two negative consequences that you will use most often in responding to sibling conflict. They are time-out and logical consequences. Let's take a quick look at each now.

Time-Out

Time-out has been well-documented over the years as an effective approach for reducing negative childhood behavior in children ages two through twelve. Please see my book *The Parent Survival Guide* for a complete description of an effective time-out procedure. When used with siblings, the use of both positive reinforcement and time-out have been found to be effective in reducing sibling fighting.[3] In one study, time-out was found to be even more effective than social skill training for reducing sibling conflict. The researchers concluded that while teaching social skills to siblings may be helpful in reducing conflict for many children, it is most effective when combined with the consistent use of time-out.[4]

FOR A LAUGH

Negative Sibling Behavior	Try	Don't Try
1. Arguing over TV channels.	No TV for rest of day.	Send them each to time-out — in different countries.
2. Fighting in back-seat of car.	Five minutes of no talking.	Flip a coin to see who to send off for adoption.
3. Calling each other names.	Fifty cent fine for each instance.	Have them hold hands, look into each other's eyes, and sing the "Barney" song.
4. Kicking each other under the table.	Time-outs or loss of meal.	As a family, watch several episodes of *The Simpsons* to see how brothers and sisters are supposed to act.
5. Arguing over what to name the puppy you might get.	Have them devise a way to choose a name (pick from a hat, each give two names, have parents choose).	Tell them that if they really want a new puppy, one of them will have to go.

When more than one sibling is treating the other disrespectfully, they each can be sent to separate time-outs. This means that you will need to have more than one time-out spot at your disposal. Time-out is helpful in squelching sibling fighting because it brings the negative interaction to an immediate end, as both children are sent off to their time-outs. This gives them each a chance to cool down and think, and increases the chance of a more productive discussion after the time-outs are over.

Logical Consequences

As we have previously discussed, when siblings treat each other respectfully, one of the benefits is the ability to engage in many desired privileges. When they treat each other disrespectfully, those privileges will be lost. While a variety of privileges can be taken away, it is always best to remove privileges that are logically related to the sibling misbehavior. For example, if your children are fighting while watching TV, the TV should be immediately turned off until they come up with an appropriate solution, or they may lose TV privileges for the rest of the day.

During a counseling session with twelve-year-old Bobby and fifteen-year-old George, the subject turned to their frequent fights over the computer.

"When I'm on the computer," Bobby began, "he comes up to me and starts shouting at me, telling me that I've been on for too long when I just got on."

"You're always on the computer, and you never set the timer," George retorted.

"Yeah, but you don't have to shout at me," Bobby said.

"And you don't have to tell me to shut up," George shot back.

"Well, that's when Dad comes in and shouts at both of us," Bobby said, grimacing.

"Why doesn't he just turn the computer off?" I asked. "If you're both being disrespectful to each other about the computer, I don't understand why anyone is using the computer at all."

Both boys fell silent and stared at me with a deer-in-the-headlights gaze. It had never dawned on them that their disrespectful behavior while on the computer could actually result in losing their own computer privileges. They were too busy trying to get each other into trouble. Their father had been responding to their disrespectful behavior by shouting at them, which resulted in postponing their disrespect until he left the room, when it could be continued more covertly. Much more effective would have been the logical consequence of Dad respectfully informing both boys that because they had chosen to handle their computer dispute disrespectfully, the computer would now be turned off. After I shared this approach with Bobby and George's parents, I was informed a few weeks later that the boys' arguing on the computer had decreased dramatically.

FIVE KEYS FOR APPLYING SIBLING CONSEQUENCES

In your effort to reduce negative sibling behavior, the way you administer negative consequences is just as important as the negative consequences themselves. Everything you do must work together to deliver an effective knockout blow to the negative sibling behavior. Here are five simple keys that will increase your effectiveness in teaching your children that negative sibling behavior doesn't pay off.

A Quick Response

If negative sibling behavior is designed to elicit some type of payoff, your job is to eliminate that payoff entirely. This is most effectively done by responding *immediately* when your children launch into disrespectful sibling behavior. Their negative behavior is a clear signal that they have failed to put their positive communication, problem-solving, and survival skills to work and have chosen instead to treat each other disrespectfully.

The lesson that needs to be learned is that handling a sibling conflict disrespectfully works out bad, and it works out bad *fast!* When Samuel and Joey start talking disrespectfully while shooting baskets in the driveway (e.g., "You're a lousy shot!"), there is no need to let this turn into a duel of insults that will build up hurtful resentment. *Immediately* pull both boys over to the side and either help them express their thoughts and feelings more respectfully, or administer a negative consequence (such as a time-out or taking a break from basketball) to whomever is unwilling to do so.

> Mom: "Hey, you guys, both of you come over here. Samuel, I heard you call Joey a lousy shot. Can you tell me why you said that?"
>
> Samuel: "He's always missing and shooting the ball behind the basket into the bushes. Then I have to go get it."
>
> Joey: "But the basket is too high."

Samuel: "It is not. You've made it before."

Mom: "Okay, guys, I get the picture. Samuel, was it respectful to tell Joey that he is a lousy shot?"

Samuel: "No, I guess not."

Mom: "Right, it wasn't, and if I hear you say something like that again, basketball will be over for you and you'll be in time-out. Do you understand?"

Samuel: "Yes, Mom."

Mom: "Okay. Good. Now, what do you say to Joey?"

Samuel: "Sorry for calling you a lousy shot. But, Mom, do I always have to get the ball?"

Mom: "No, you don't. *(Mom puts her hands on each boy's shoulder.)* Samuel, that was a nice job saying you're sorry to Joey. Now, let's put our heads together and see if we can figure out a way to have fun playing basketball together. Joey, if you shoot the ball and it goes into the bushes, who do you think should get it?"

I have seen many sibling disputes respectfully and creatively worked out, in large part due to early intervention on the part of the parents. In this example, Mom first focused on Samuel's disrespectful *behavior* (e.g., no comparing or labeling) and then helped both boys move to problem solving in order to find a good solution. As a result of her quick response, the boys were able to stop the negative spiral before it had gained too much momentum.

When you intervene early, the sibling conflict has often not had enough time to build up a lot of steam. This means that your children are more capable of expressing themselves respectfully and being flexible in arriving at a solution. If they choose not to do so, then they will earn an immediate negative consequence. Either way, they learn that choosing to treat their sibling disrespectfully is a fast one-way ticket down a short dead-end street.

Matter-of-Fact Delivery

Lecturing and shouting are two of the most unproductive responses you can make when addressing sibling conflict. Your goal is to deliver your negative consequences in a clear, matter-of-fact manner. No fireworks, no big emotional display. Just let your children know what they did and what is going to happen as a result. After all, your children are the ones about to go to time-out or lose a privilege, not you.

While there will be occasions where your understandable frustration will seep through, make sure your children see you express this frustration in a respectful way. This is your golden opportunity to let your children see what it looks like when frustration is handled the right way. If your child has earned a time-out, administer it immediately and talk with your child about the misbehavior only *after* the time-out is completed. If your child has earned a logical consequence, then you can discuss the misbehavior whenever your child is able to discuss it respectfully. If your child argues or becomes disrespectful during this discussion, discontinue the discussion until it can be handled respectfully. Administer an additional time-out if needed.

Examples:

Mom: "Timmy, it is never okay to hit your brother. That just earned you a time-out. Let's go."

Dad: "What are you two fighting about? I'll tell you what, Jill, I want you to sit in this chair. Sammy, I want you to sit right here. There will be absolutely no talking. I want you to think about what you want to say and how to say it in a respectful way. I'll give you about two minutes to sit there and think, and then we'll talk."

Mom: "Okay, guys, if you are going to fight when you play with the cars, then the cars will have to go away for a while. We'll see if we can try it again some other time."

Dad: "Sorry, the TV is off now. If you girls are going to argue and talk disrespectfully about choosing channels, then we just won't watch at all. If you both act respectfully from now on, we'll see if we can try the TV again after dinner. Now, can I help you two talk through this problem the right way?"

Watch for Disrespect

Some sibling disputes are the result of both children acting disrespectfully, while other disputes involve one child acting disrespectfully and the other trying to be respectful. Your goal is always to reward respectful behavior and provide negative consequences for disrespectful behavior. If both children are treating each other disrespectfully, then consequences will be immediately given to both. However, if in your best judgment, it appears that one child is doing her best to handle a situation respectfully (as you have practiced in your family times), then that child should not be given a negative consequence.

In some situations, you will simply have to use your best judgment and rely on past experience as to who was likely being respectful or disrespectful. However, if you are consistently practicing positive communication, problem solving, and survival skills, and rehearsing respectful behavior in your family times, then it will become increasingly clear to you when a child is trying to put those skills to use. Remember, it is your children's job to handle things so respectfully that there will be no confusion.

Address Relationships

As we discussed in Section One, each member of your family is valuable, both to God and to your family. Therefore, it is never acceptable for your children to purposely hurt each other with their words or actions. When a person chooses to hurt a family member, it is that person's responsibility to take the first step in restoring the relationship that they have hurt. God places a high value on relationships, and your family should do the same. Part of that repair effort needs to include an apology by the offending person.

> Dad: "Anthony and David, what do you guys think about how you both were talking to each other just now?"
>
> Anthony: "Not so good, I guess."
>
> Dad: "David?"
>
> David: "Well, he started it . . ."
>
> Dad: "Guys, remember what we talked about in our family times. The thing that counts is that we treat each other respectfully, even if we disagree about something. Do you guys remember that?"
>
> David: "Yeah."

Dad: "We decided that even if we are mad, God does not want us to hurt each other with our words or actions. I think you guys were both hurtful just now with your words. What do you think?"

Anthony: "Yeah."

David: "I guess so."

Dad: "Well, what did we say we wanted to do in our family if we hurt someone with our words or actions?"

Anthony: "Apologize?"

Dad: "That's right. Because the person who did the hurting needs to help repair the relationship they hurt. *(Placing his hands on both boys' shoulders)* And right now I think both of you said some hurtful things to each other. So, how can we help fix things up?"

Anthony: *(looking down)* "I'm sorry for what I said."

Dad: "Anthony, I'd like you to look at David when you tell him that."

Anthony: *(making eye contact with David)* "I'm sorry."

David: *(briefly looking at Anthony)* "Yeah, me too."

Dad: *(putting his arm around both boys)* "Hey, I'm proud of you boys for how you just handled this. You were both very respectful when you apologized, and you really helped our family just now. I can't wait to tell Mom what you guys did; she'll be proud of you too. Now, let's see if we can find a solution to this problem, respectfully."

Make sure that your child does not think he is apologizing for feeling angry. In some situations, he may have every reason to be angry. *An apology is necessary only if your child was disrespectful to his sibling with his words or behaviors.* In many situations, both children will need to apologize for their role in the sibling conflict. Then, help them think of how they both could have handled the situation more respectfully.

Apologizing when a relationship is hurt is a good practice to begin when your children are young. In a rare instance, a child may refuse to apologize in a moment of heated anger. If this happens, do not try to force it (indeed, you can't). Give him some time to cool down and let him know that you'll revisit the issue later. If he still refuses to apologize for his disrespectful behavior after you have discussed it again, then calmly let him know that he will experience a negative consequence as a result (e.g., no computer for two weeks). The negative consequence can be terminated whenever he decides to apologize. This sends the message loud and clear: relationships are top priority in your family.

Apologizing and taking responsibility for one's actions are excellent topics for family time discussions and should be repeated as necessary. You will also help your children learn the value of taking responsibility for their own behavior and prioritizing relationships by making sure that you apologize to them when you make mistakes or treat them disrespectfully.

Be Consistent

There is nothing like consistency to help children learn where the lines are drawn. Phillip, whom I spoke of at the opening of Step Eight, chose to treat his sister disrespectfully because his parents, Bill and Gail, had not *consistently* responded to his negative behavior in an effective way. Sometimes they ignored it; other times they gave him a reprimand. Occasionally Phillip would actually get into trouble. However, the odds were that the payoff would outweigh the cost of the negative sibling behavior, and Phillip knew it. So the behavior continued.

The rest of Phillip's story goes like this. After several sessions talking with Bill and Gail about their approach to Phillip and Katrina's negative sibling behavior, they became more consistent in their responses. As they began to do this, things began to change for Phillip. He no longer got away with his negative behavior nearly as often, and the consequences were now both immediate and effective. Phillip began going to time-out more frequently and losing special privileges, such as his electronic games, when he acted disrespectfully toward Katrina. The same rules and consequences were applied to Katrina as well.

While it was difficult initially, Bill and Gail slowly turned the tide. Gail's parents had been extremely strict when she was a child, and because of her emotional reaction to this, she found it difficult to hold firm limits with her children. Gail was afraid her children would harbor negative feelings toward her if she held firm on her expectations. However, with Bill's help and her willingness to confront this leftover baggage from her childhood, Gail made great strides in her ability to consistently enforce their new respectful family rules.

As Bill and Gail held firm and his negative sibling behavior consistently worked out poorly for him, Phillip was ushered into a new reality. Now, the only behavior that brought a

KEYS FOR APPLYING NEGATIVE CONSEQUENCES

1. A quick response
2. Matter-of-fact delivery
3. Watch for disrespect
4. Address relationships
5. Be consistent

payoff was respectful behavior. And Gail learned that she did not lose her children's love by requiring respectful behavior. In fact, the opposite occurred. Gail was instrumental in making her family a place where close sibling and family relationships had a chance to grow.

As Phillip practiced positive communication and problem-solving skills with me in sessions and with his family at home, his skills improved and he began to get the big picture. His family had become a family where honoring God by treating others respectfully was a high and unwavering priority. As Phillip began to live within those guidelines, he became a much happier boy and started to lose privileges less often. The time came when I no longer had to work with Phillip. He had learned that following God's commands to treat others as he would like to be treated was indeed a golden rule after all.

QUESTIONS FOR REFLECTION

1. List five negative sibling behaviors that you would like to see your children display less often.

2. How quickly do you usually respond to negative sibling behavior? Do you think it would help turn things around if you responded more quickly?

3. Which of the Five Keys for Applying Negative Consequences do you need to work on the most?

4. List five privileges that your children can lose as the result of negative sibling behavior.

5. Choose two effective time-out spots that can be used if both children need to be sent to time-out at the same time.

6. Read Proverbs 29:17 and Hebrews 12:11. Write down a plan for using positive *and* negative consequences to discipline (or teach) your children to treat each other respectfully.

Behavior to increase: _____

How I will reinforce this behavior: _____

Behavior to decrease:_____

Negative consequences I will use: _____

PRAYER SUGGESTIONS

Close this time by asking God to help you respond to negative sibling behavior in a way that teaches your children the right lessons. Pray that God will help you to model respectful behavior in every discipline situation and to always treat your children with value and respect. Thank God for allowing you to parent the children he has given you for a short time and ask him to continue to shape you into the parent he wants you to be.

PRACTICE MAKES PERFECT

1. What would be an effective response if your children were arguing about who should get the last cookie?

2. While walking past the playroom, you overhear your children using hurtful words ("stupid," "idiot"). When should you respond?

(You can find sample responses on page 232.)

For your next family time, choose from Family Time Discussion Guides #6–8 or 11–14.

PUT THEM ON THE SAME TEAM

first met ten-year-old Mariah and her seven-year-old sister, Tammy, when I was working at a large midwest children's hospital. Ms. Jones had brought her daughters to therapy because of their inability to get along.

"They're always at each other," Ms. Jones said with an exasperated sigh. "Bickering, calling each other names, touching each other. It just wears me out. And if it's not one, it's the other one doing something just to bother her sister."

"It sounds very tiring," I reflected. "So, what do you do?"

"It doesn't seem like anything I do makes any difference," Ms. Jones answered. "I can never tell who started it. They both say the other one did. So, what am I supposed to do? Sometimes, I just say, 'You two figure it out' and walk away."

"Does that seem to help?" I asked.

"No. Pretty soon they're just at it again," came her dejected response.

Unknowingly, Ms. Jones had been caught in what I have come to call the "Sherlock Holmes trap." She was trying to solve the mystery of "Whodunit?" but she didn't have enough clues to go on. Who started it? Who hit whom first? Who called the first name? All unanswerable questions. As a result, she was seldom able to solve the mystery and felt trapped between a rock and a hard place. If she punished both children, she might punish an innocent child, which would be unfair. If she punished no one, she knew that one or both of them were getting away with murder.

ASKING THE RIGHT QUESTION

When you are caught in the Sherlock Holmes trap, the reality is that your children's problem has become your problem. They have behaved disrespectfully, and you are the one experiencing all the emotional wear and tear!

This is entirely backwards. Your job is to make your children's sibling misbehavior *their* problem, not yours. The way out of the Sherlock Holmes trap is to stop asking "whodunit?" and to start asking a different question. The only question you need to ask yourself in any sibling dispute is this: *Who is handling the situation respectfully and who is not?*

If you find that one particular child tends to instigate most of the sibling problems and the other children usually try to handle things respectfully, then you really have more of a single child problem than a sibling problem. In this case, the previous steps we have discussed should be very useful in helping each of your children learn the right lessons about behaving respectfully and responding to sibling aggravation. If your instigator does not respond to your best efforts and continues to disrupt family relationships, you should consult with a qualified child therapist.

However, for those of you who have two children who frequently instigate conflict with each other and you are never sure who started what and know very well that it could have been either of them and was probably both of them, then a team approach is for you.

THE TEAM APPROACH

When two children are in the middle of a sibling conflict and are using every trick in the book to blame it on each other, think of them as being on opposing teams. Each of them is trying to win by making the other one lose.

You have the power to change this. Whether they like it or not, you can put them on the same team. And when they are on the same team, everything changes. They either both swim, or they both sink. They either both win, or they both lose. Like it or not, they're teammates, and the sooner they start acting like it, the better it will be for both of them.

This is the approach I took with Mariah and Tammy. They were both regularly instigating negative sibling behavior with each other, and we needed to get Ms. Jones out of the Sherlock Holmes trap.

"I think you guys need to be on the same team," I declared, putting my notepad down and looking both girls straight in the eye.

They both stared back at me with wide-open eyes, having no idea what I was talking about but afraid that whatever it was, it might require them to change.

"What do you mean?" Ms. Jones asked.

"Well, right now they're on different teams," I explained, "with one of them always trying to beat the other. If Mariah gets in trouble, then Tammy wins. If Tammy gets in trouble, then Mariah wins. That's not how families are supposed to work.

"They need to be on the same team, and if they treat each other respectfully, then it will work out good for both of them. If they treat each other disrespectfully, then it will work out bad for both of them. They will have fun, or be sad—as a team. And the more respectful they are, the more fun there will be."

"I see," said Ms. Jones, beginning to get the picture. "But how do I do that?"

"Girls, listen up." I smiled. "I think you're going to like this. It's going to be a lot of fun and it's going to help you get along a lot better. How does that sound?"

They both nodded their approval.

FIVE STEPS FOR BUILDING YOUR TEAM

We proceeded to explain and develop a team approach for Mariah and Tammy. There are five steps for using the team approach. I'll explain each step now and show you how the steps worked with Mariah and Tammy.

1. Explain that your children are now on the same team.

In the preceding paragraphs, I have demonstrated most of the first step. Simply explain that the children are going to be on the same team and that when they treat each other respectfully, they will have more fun and when they treat each other disrespectfully, they will lose privileges. But they will have fun or lose privileges together, as a team. And the more respectfully they both treat each other, the more fun they will both have.

2. Make a reward menu for each child.

The second step begins with making a small reward menu for each child. This is a list of fun activities or privileges that each child would like to earn as the result of positive sibling behavior. Each child can have her own reward menu as they may be motivated to work for different privileges.

Example:

> **Me:** "Now that you guys know what we're going to do, let's start by making a list of fun things that you can do if you treat each other respectfully and get along. We can make a list for each of you. Mariah, let's make yours first. What are a couple special fun things that you would like to do?"
>
> **Mariah:** "Maybe get a new doll?"
>
> **Me:** "If that's okay with your mom, we can put it on the list. Mom?"
>
> **Ms. Jones:** "Sure, that's fine."
>
> **Me:** "Great. How about if we make some things on the list little, and have a few bigger ones?"
>
> **Mariah:** "Sure."
>
> **Me:** "Okay, so a new doll . . . that would probably be on the big list. Now, what else can we put on your list? *(After completing Mariah's list)* "That's a great list. Now, let's make a list for Tammy. Tammy, are you ready?"
>
> **Tammy:** "I'm ready."
>
> **Me:** "Good. All right. Let's think of a couple fun things you can put on your list."
>
> **Tammy:** "I'd like a new doll too. And maybe I could ask Alicia over to play."
>
> **Me:** "Mom, are those okay?"
>
> **Ms. Jones:** "Sure, those are fine."

3. Decide how many points the team will start with each day.

Start your team with anywhere between five and ten points a day. The more conflict there is, the higher number of points you should start them with, so that they will be able to still have some points left when the day is through. You want your children to earn some points so that they have a chance to earn rewards from their menu.

REWARD MENU

Mariah	Tammy
15 points	*15 points*
Making cookies with Mom	Alicia over to play
Choose movie for family night	Choose game for family night
Stay up thirty minutes later	Stay up thirty minutes later
25 points	*25 points*
A new doll	A new doll
A trip to special candy store	Have pizza for dinner
Go to family movie	A packet of colored pens

Example:

Me: "Okay, you guys, your team will start out with five points each day. That means that every day when you wake up, your team will already have five points. All you have to do is open your eyes and—boom!—five points! How does that sound?"

Both girls: *(nod their approval)*

Me: "Now, we want you to keep all of your points, because you can use them to earn the fun privileges on your reward menu. Now, get this. At the end of each day, however many points your team still has, that's how many points go into your individual point banks. For example, if you guys do a great job getting along and being respectful to each other, your team would keep all five points. That means that five points go into your bank *(points to Mariah)* and five points go into yours too *(points to Tammy)*.

"Then your team starts out with five more points the next morning, and hopefully you can keep all of those. But let's say your team lost one point because you argued with each other. Then you would only have four points left. But if you were respectful for the rest of the day, then your team would keep those four points. You both get to save up your points and use them to buy things from your reward menu. Sound like fun?"

Tammy: "I can't wait to get a new doll!"

Mariah: "Me too."

4. Clearly define how the team can keep or lose their points.

The next step is to let your children know what they have to do to keep their points and exactly what behaviors will cause them to lose points. Basically speaking, it is disrespectful behavior that will cost them points, while respectful behavior will help them keep their points.

You will aid your children by specifically listing the types of respectful behaviors that will help their team and disrespectful behaviors that will cost their team points. The lists should be specific and include the types of negative sibling behaviors you want to see reduced and their positive, respectful counterparts. Look at the sidebar below for an example of what these lists might look like.

Let your children know that their team will lose a point each time they are both involved in the disrespectful behaviors you have listed. They

RESPECTFUL BEHAVIORS

(will help you keep points)
1. Sharing
2. Taking turns
3. Talking respectfully
4. Encouraging comments
5. Getting parent if you're not sure how to solve a problem

DISRESPECTFUL BEHAVIORS

(will cost you points)
1. Hitting, kicking, pushing, etc.
2. Name-calling
3. Arguing
4. Shouting

will also each go directly to time-out and, if appropriate, a logical consequence will also be given. For example, if the girls begin to fight and call each other names while playing together with their dolls, then their team will lose one point, each girl will go directly to time-out, and their dolls may be removed for the rest of the day.

The only exception to this is if one child is *clearly* disrespectful while the other *clearly* responds in a respectful way. In this case, only the child who acted disrespectfully will receive appropriate negative consequences. Because the other child responded appropriately, the team does *not* lose a point. Instead, that child's respectful response saved the team point.

Example:

>Me: "Now, we want you guys to know exactly what to do so that you can keep all of your points. So, let's make a list of the kind of respectful behaviors that will help you get along and help your team keep its points. *(Make respectful behavior list.)*
>
>"Good. Now, let's make a list of the kinds of behaviors that will get you guys into trouble and make your team lose a point. These are disrespectful behaviors. Can you think of one we should put on the list?"
>
>Mariah: "Hitting."
>
>Me: "That sounds right. What do you think, Mom?"
>
>Ms. Jones: "That sounds good to me."
>
>Me: "What about you, Tammy?"
>
>Tammy: "I agree."
>
>Me: "Okay. Hitting is on the list. We should also include any kind of touch that could hurt someone. Like pushing, kicking, and shoving, or anything else."
>
>Ms. Jones: "Yes, girls, that's right."
>
>Me: "Okay, what else should we put on our list? *(Complete disrespectful behavior list.)* All right. Now you know how to keep all your points and what kind of disrespectful behaviors will cost your team a point. You will also earn a time-out and maybe even another consequence when you do these behaviors. That's because they are disrespectful and hurt your relationships with each other. Do you understand?"

Tammy: "Yep."

Me: "Okay, there's one more thing. If one of you starts to act disrespectfully, then that person is going to get into trouble for sure. But what is the smartest thing the other person can do?"

Mariah: "Go get Mom?"

Me: "Hey, that might work just fine. If the other person acts disrespectfully to you, the smartest thing you can do is to still be respectful. That means if the other person starts to shout, what should you do, Tammy?"

Tammy: "Shout back?"

Me: "Nope. You should say what you think respectfully. That way, you won't get into trouble. Now, listen closely. If Mom thinks that one person acted disrespectfully but the other person acted *respectfully* back, then the person who was disrespectful will get into trouble, but the team *will not* lose a point and the girl who was *respectful* will not get into trouble. The girl who was respectful saved the team by being respectful! What do you think of that?"

Mariah: "That's pretty good."

Me: "Now, remember, it will be up to Mom. She's the judge and jury, so whatever she says goes. But if she thinks you were respectful, then it should work out good for you. And if you both are respectful, well then, you'll have so many points you won't know what to do with them! How does that sound, Tammy?"

Tammy: "I like it."

Me: "Me too. And when you guys come back here again, we'll practice together how to be more respectful to each other so that you'll get better and better at it. Sound okay?"

Both girls: "Okay."

5. As sibling behavior improves, slowly fade the plan out.

Keep track of how many points the team keeps every day. As your children's behavior improves, you will find that they will begin to keep most of their points. When this positive behavior is sustained for about four weeks, tell your children that they are doing so well that they don't need the points to help them as much as they used to. Then reduce their starting number of daily points by one or two (e.g., from five to three). Now they will have to work slightly longer to gain enough points for a reward menu item.

Make sure that you are rehearsing respectful sibling behaviors with your children, using the communication, problem-solving, and sibling survival skills we discussed in Section Two. Also, remember to provide each child with plenty of specific positive attention and point out the connection between their respectful sibling behaviors and the resulting positive results, as we discussed in Step Eight. This will help your children be more aware of the many positive results their respectful sibling behavior brings *even without the points*, and makes fading the team approach easier.

Continue to slowly reduce the starting number of daily team points as your children's positive sibling behavior improves. At some point, you can decide together as a family to discontinue the team approach altogether. Remind your children that they have gotten much better at treating each other respectfully and no longer need points to help them. Have them list the many positive results that come from respectful sibling behavior (there are many!), and congratulate them on a job well done.

About four months later . . .

Me:	"Well, guys, how are you doing?"
Ms. Jones:	"I think they're doing good!"
Me:	"That's great news. What do you guys think?"
Mariah:	"We're doing good."
Tammy:	"Yeah, we're keeping lots of our points."
Me:	"Are you really? How many points is your team keeping each day?"
Ms. Jones:	"They're keeping four or five points most of the time now. Sometimes, they'll lose a few more, but not very often."
Me:	"Wow! That's great! You guys have really learned some good lessons about how to be respectful. Hey, let me ask you this. What are some respectful things that you do to each other now that help your team to keep its points?"

Tammy: "We don't shout as much."

Mariah: "And we take turns better too."

Me: "Really. Is that so, Mom?"

Ms. Jones: "Yes, I'd say they do both of those things better than they used to."

Me: "Well, congratulations. Which do you think is more fun, being respectful or disrespectful?"

Mariah: (with a smile) "Respectful."

Tammy: "I think so too."

WITH THREE OR MORE SIBLINGS

Many of you will never have to use the team approach with your children, but will instead address sibling conflict by preparing your family soil, planting effective communication, problem solving, and survival skills, and providing the right learning environment for each of your children. Remember, the team approach is specifically designed for the situation where you have *two siblings who both instigate sibling conflict with each other on a frequent and relatively equal basis.* It is not effective to place more than two siblings on a team, as the team could lose a point when one of the siblings is not even in the house, creating a sense of unfairness in the whole approach.

If you have three or more children, and two of them are regularly aggravating each other, let those two children know that even though your whole family is a team, they are going to be a "special team" for a short time, to help them learn to be more respectful to each other. You can make different teams anytime you need to. Then, proceed with the steps I have previously outlined. Pay close attention to your children's progress, and as soon as their behavior improves or only *one* sibling regularly instigates conflict, then you can discontinue the team approach and rely on the approaches we have previously discussed.

If your other children feel left out because they don't have a reward menu, you can do two things. First, remind them of the many natural rewards they *already* experience as the result of being respectful. This is actually much better than having to earn points to have these privileges. Second, if your other children really want a reward menu too, you can tell them that for every respectful day they have, you will place an X on a calendar for each child. Once a child has earned ten X's, he or she can have a special privilege that you both agree to.

QUESTIONS FOR REFLECTION

1. Do you have two children who regularly instigate conflict with each other?

2. Do you think the team approach (when combined with the other steps) will help teach your children the types of loving and respectful behaviors listed in Galatians 5:22 and Colossians 3:12–14?

3. If you used the team approach, what other approaches (that we have discussed in earlier steps) would you use as well?

4. If you have more than two children, how do you think your other children would respond if you used the team approach with two of your children? How would you handle this situation?

PRAYER SUGGESTIONS

Close this time by asking God to help everyone in your family learn to treat each other as his precious workmanship. If you are considering using a team approach with two of your children, pray that God will help those two children develop good habits of treating each other in the respectful way he desires them to. Ask God to help you lead the way for your family by providing a living example of how he wants us to treat each other.

PRACTICE MAKES PERFECT

1. If you have two children who frequently instigate conflict with each other, the team approach may be quite helpful. Make a list of the negative behaviors that you would like to reduce.

2. Make a list of the positive, respectful behaviors that will help your children keep their team points.

   (You can find sample responses on page 233.)

For your next family time, choose from Family Time Discussion Guides #6–8 or #11–14.

SEEING YOUR ROSES THROUGH THE THORNS

Throughout this book, we have taken glimpses at the sibling relationships of Mitchell and Kayla; Melanie and Heidi; Alex and Katie; Danny and Kevin; and Eric, Alan, and Molly, among others.

There is one thing that most of these siblings have in common: I *used* to see them regularly in my office. I still have contact with a few of these families today as the children are still in the process of learning how to treat each other respectfully. Some of these children have additional temperamental, neurological, or family challenges that require extra time and attention to help them get on the right track.

Most of these siblings, however, no longer need to see me because they have learned how to treat each other more respectfully. Their parents have taken new steps toward creating strong family bonds and a nurturing family soil. These children have learned important living-together skills and have begun to integrate them into their daily lives. Their family environment is now one that reinforces respectful behavior and provides effective negative consequences for disrespectful behavior. In short, their sibling relationships have moved closer to becoming what God intended them to be.

TYING IT ALL TOGETHER

When you plant a flower, each part of the growth process is important. If you just prepare the soil, but don't plant the seed, you will have a healthy pile of dirt. If you plant the seed in unhealthy soil, it doesn't stand much chance of taking root. If you prepare the soil and plant the seed, but provide the wrong environment, your flower will not last for long. In the same way, *each* part of this process is necessary if you want to cultivate healthy sibling relationships.

Julie was tearful as she sat in my office and reached across the end table for a tissue. We had been talking about her children's behavior and the disrespectful environment that had invaded her once happy family. "I just don't know where to start," she said, shaking her head. "Robby gets angry at Bryan so easily, and they both just seem to annoy each other all the time. And now, Kaitlyn is starting to pick up some of their bad habits. We've got to do something, and quick!"

Julie is exactly right. She and her husband, Dan, need to renourish their damaged family soil by starting regular family times and reconnecting with each of their children individually. They need to teach their children the Family Respect Rule and show them what respectful behavior *really* looks like.

But it doesn't stop there. Julie and Dan also need to teach their children positive communication, problem solving, and survival skills to help them handle their sibling conflicts more productively. They need to practice these skills together as a family in order to build up their children's good habits to take the place of the bad. They also need to create a family environment that reinforces respectful sibling behavior and ensures that disrespectful sibling behavior never pays off.

The good news is that Julie and Dan can begin working on *each* part of the growth process right away. One part does not have to be perfect before the others can be started. In fact, all three parts of this process work together as a complete unit, with each part helping the others to be successful. The more bonded together their family relationships are, the easier it will be to teach important living-together skills. The better their children get at their living-together skills, the more likely they are to develop close sibling relationships. And as respectful sibling behavior is reinforced and disrespectful behavior is gradually diminished, the more their children will enjoy interacting together.

THROUGH A PARENT'S EYES

During the course of writing this book, I began to ask parents if they would share their experiences of parenting siblings with me (and with you). The comments I received from these gracious parents were refreshingly realistic and unexpectedly inspiring.

Almost all the parents I talked with described the experience of having multiple children as being positive, even if they had one or more children that were difficult. Clearly, these are parents that love each of their children very much. However, every one of them told me that their children often argued or fought over everyday issues. Here are the types of sibling conflict that they reported:

Our children . . .

> fight over toys
> don't share
> call each other names
> can't take turns
> tease each other
> fight about who goes first
> are jealous of each other
> want all my attention
> argue about which toy belongs to whom
> annoy each other

Sound familiar?

On the brighter side, each parent indicated that having more than one child was a wonderful blessing. When I asked them what they felt the advantages of having more than one child were, here a few of the responses I received:

The children . . .

> get to play with each other
> learn how to share
> have more fun
> have a built-in playmate
> develop close relationships
> learn to be less focused on material things
> learn to be considerate of other's feelings
> learn to work through disagreements
> learn life lessons of sacrifice, praying for each other, comforting
>   each other
> work through conflict with each other

learn to think about what is best for the entire family, instead of just themselves

learn how to get along when someone is annoying them

These parents also described the aspects of raising siblings that they felt were most difficult. I immediately related to these frustrations, having experienced them myself many times. See if any of these frustrations sound familiar:

- Not being able to give each child as much attention as you would like
- Making negative comparisons between your children
- Trying to be fair to everyone
- Not having enough time for each of your children
- Explaining to younger children why they can't have the same privileges as the older ones
- Always being the referee
- Scheduling each child's activities
- Handling the noise level
- Meeting the unique needs of each child
- Adjusting your parenting style for different children
- Keeping your energy up to deal with each child
- Being consistent

When I asked parents what interventions they have found to be the most successful at helping their children to get along better, here is the list they gave me:

- Enforcing time-outs (for both if needed)
- Giving positive reinforcement for positive behavior
- Teaching and role-playing positive behavior
- Having a regular family night
- Emphasizing the importance of family relationships
- Having both siblings lose a privilege
- Not intervening until they have tried to work it out
- Separating the children
- Having the children hug after an argument
- Insisting on respectful behavior

- Having each child sit on a separate chair, fold their hands, and calm down before trying to resolve a conflict
- Using negative consequences for disrespectful behavior
- Assigning extra chores as a negative consequence
- Giving immediate praise and encouragement when they see one child show love or kindness to another
- Pointing out opportunities for one child to show kindness to another
- Orchestrating situations where there is a positive sibling outcome

THROUGH A SIBLING'S EYES

I have also had the opportunity to ask a number of children what they think about the pros and cons of having siblings. Here are some of the responses I got when I asked about the more difficult side of sibling life:

The hardest thing about having a brother or sister is . . .

- Crying and screaming
- Pulls my hair
- Taking turns
- I have to share
- Tells me wrong answers on purpose
- Deciding who gets to sit in the front
- I get less attention if she's sick
- Sings annoying songs
- I have to clean up a mess he/she made
- I get blamed for something he/she did
- Embarrasses me when my friends are over

On the brighter side, here are some of the reasons these children gave for why they like having siblings:

- We have fun playing together.
- I like to hang out with him and his friends.
- I have someone to talk to.
- Sometimes we agree on things.
- We can wear the same clothes.

- We have things in common.
- She can help me with homework.
- You always have someone to play with.

Reading these comments reminds me that the quality of your family life is not a chance event. When you follow God's principles, you *can* "train your children in the way they should go," as Solomon encouraged us to do (Proverbs 22:6). You *can* create a healthy and nourishing family soil that will provide the foundation for healthy sibling relationships. You *can* teach your children practical living-together skills that will help them treat others the way God wants them to. You *can* provide a family environment that teaches your children that being respectful to each other is always worth the effort it takes.

If you incorporate the ten steps outlined in this book into your family life, you and your children will reap the benefits of them. Don't get me wrong—using these ten steps does not guarantee a conflict-free family environment. But it does mean that you can use those conflicts to help your children learn to value their family relationships and experience the benefits that come from following God's blueprint for family life.

SEEING YOUR ROSES

Someone once said, "You can complain that rosebushes have thorns, or be thankful that thornbushes have roses." In the same way, it is easy to become overfocused on the challenges of parenting and forget the joy your children bring to your life and the great potential that lies inside each of them.

Here is an exercise I challenge you to do with me. Close your eyes and picture your children getting along together. Now, this may be a new picture for some of you, but hang in there with me. On a scale of one to ten (ten being best), imagine them at an eight or nine. Hear them laughing together while they play cooperatively with their toys. Envision them talking respectfully and encouraging each other when one loses at a game. Picture your family having fun together during a family game night and engaging in meaningful family discussion about God's Word and other important life issues. In your mind's eye, see a sibling conflict take place, but watch each of your children make an effort to handle the situation with respectful words and actions.

Now, ask yourself this question: *What does God want for my family?* I'd like to suggest to you that you have just imagined it. Not a perfect family, where no one makes mistakes. But a family where everyone is working toward becoming the person that God made him or her to be and a family where everyone is learning how to treat each other with value and respect.

Listen to these encouraging words. "'For I know the plans I have for you,' declares the LORD, 'plans to prosper you and not to harm you, plans to give you hope and a future'" (Jeremiah 29:11).

I think this is a wonderful verse for every parent. What do you think God's plans are for your family? What are his plans for your children? I believe the imagination exercise you just completed gives you a glimpse into God's plan for your family. He desires for your family to live out his principles in your daily family life (Deuteronomy 6:4–9). He wants your children to experience the lifelong benefits of following his commands. He wants them to learn to handle the challenges of being siblings in a way that builds healthy family relationships and reflects his holy character in their lives.

You are an integral part of God's plan for your children. He has placed you in your family, knowing that you have what it takes to teach your children what they need to learn. God is able to complete what he has promised, and he has promised to help you become the parent your children need. Remember Paul's encouraging words: "I can do everything through him who gives me strength" (Philippians 4:13).

I encourage you to look past the sibling conflict and disrespectful behavior and see the loving, unique personalities that God has planted in each of your children. Remember that in your eyes and words, your children see their reflection. The reflection they see will influence who they think they are and what they think they can become.

Make sure the reflection your children see in your eyes and hear in your voice reminds them that they are God's special children, whom he has filled with potential. Help them to see themselves as God sees them, by remembering to look at them as God looks at them. If you are willing to get your hands dirty and do the hard work of preparing your family soil, planting the seeds of healthy relational skills, and providing an environment that encourages respectful choices, then you will help your children grow and blossom into the beautiful flowers that God had in mind when he created siblings.

QUESTIONS FOR REFLECTION

1. As you reflect on the three parts of the growth process (e.g., prepare the soil, plant the seed, provide the right environment), which parts currently need the most attention in your family?

2. What steps do you need to take to get all three parts of the growth process working in your family at the same time?

3. How have you seen the three parts of the growth process affect each other in your family?

4. As you read the comments from parents, which comments do you identify with the most?

5. Have you ever fallen into the trap of focusing too much on the "thorns" and failing to see the roses?

6. How can you adjust your perspective to see more clearly the roses God has given you?

7. Read Jeremiah 29:11. How does this verse apply to your family? What do you think God's plan or hope is for your children? For you as a parent? For your family?

PRAYER SUGGESTIONS

Close this time by reflecting on the changes your family has made as you have put these ten steps to work. Ask God to point out changes that still need to be made and areas that need to be addressed, both in yourself and in your children. Pray that God will help you to be the leader your family needs by becoming the disciple he desires. As always, thank him for the roses he has given you and for the boundless potential that lies within each one.

For your next family time, use Family Time Discussion Guide #15: Our Family Checkup.

FAMILY TIME
DISCUSSION GUIDES

Here are fifteen Family Time Discussion Guides that you can use to teach your children the valuable principles and lessons that you have learned throughout this book. Use these guides in the way that fits your family the best. Feel free to shorten or lengthen the discussions and activities to customize them for your family. Use these guides as often as you need to teach these important lessons and rehearse them together as a family. Keep your family times fun and interactive, remembering that the more enjoyable they are, the more your children will look forward to them and learn from them.

OUR FIRST FAMILY TIME

*Begin by doing a fun family activity together, such as play-
ing a game, visiting a pet store, or getting some ice cream. You
can get other ideas from the list on page 36. Then gather together in your family room and have fun with this first family
discussion.*

YOU WILL NEED:

- Paper and pen
- One or two packages of M&Ms
- A Bible

INTRODUCE FAMILY TIME

Begin by saying: **We're going to start meeting together like this
every week, and we're going to call it our Family Time. This is
a time for us to have fun together and grow together as a family. We can talk about anything we want. We'll learn some lessons
from God's Word in a fun way and talk about how we can get
along with each other and make our family the best family it
can be. What do you guys think?**

ACTIVITY: FAMILY TIME ACTIVITIES LIST

Say: **We're going to start our family times today by making a
few important lists. When we have a family time, we'll usually
start by doing something fun together, and then we'll talk
together afterwards. So, let's make a list of some fun things we
can do during our family times. We can always add other things
to the list later.** *(Make a list of fun activities. Don't include an activity on the
list unless you are willing to do it.)* **Hey, that's a super list.**

ACTIVITY: DISCUSSION TOPICS LIST

Say: Now, I'd like to know what kind of things we all would like to talk about during our family times. What kind of things do you think would be important to talk about? *(Write down ideas.)*

Read one or more of the following: Galatians 5:22–23, Ephesians 4:25–27, Colossians 3:12–15. *Ask:* What ideas do you get from these verses about things we can talk about?

(Remember the categories of family devotions, personal/family issues, character traits, and life skills. If your children have difficulty coming up with ideas, suggest topics from these four categories.) Say: That's a great list. I can't wait to talk together about those things.

DISCUSSION: OUR FAMILY

Say: Now, for our first few family times, we are going to talk about how we all get along as a family. We'll talk about how we get along with each other, how you guys *(point to children)* get along with each other, and how we can make our family the kind of family God wants it to be. How does that sound?

Say: Let's go around in a circle and all take turns saying one thing we like about our family. When you give your answer, you get an M&M. Let's see, who would like to go first? *(If a child has difficulty with this, encourage him to finish this sentence: "One thing I like about my family is _____.")*. Go clockwise around the circle two or three times. When a child gives an answer, toss him a single M&M.

Say: That was great. Now, who can tell me what we just learned about our family? *(Let the children take turns recalling some of the comments that have been made.)*

ACTIVITY: FAMILY DECISION TIME

Say: Okay, now it's time for a family decision. Let's look at our list of fun things to do for family time and pick one to do for our next family time. *(Have one family member read through the list.)* Remember, we'll probably get to all of them sooner or later. Which one would you guys like to do next time? *(If it becomes difficult to choose an activity, quickly suggest a few ways of deciding: Let the parent choose, take a vote, take turns choosing—starting with the youngest, parent chooses two activities and kids do rock/paper/scissors to pick the final one, etc. If your children have trouble with this, immediately tell them that the parents will talk it over and decide upon the activity for next time. Then close the discussion and move on.)*

CLOSING PRAYER

Say: **One of the most important things we can do in our family times is to pray together. Today, let's each say a short prayer, asking God to bless our family times and make us into the kind of family he wants us to be.** *(Choose one person to start and go around in a circle, with a parent saying the final prayer. If a child feels uncomfortable praying out loud, don't force it or turn it into an issue. Quietly prompt the next person in the circle to go ahead and pray. Over time, all of your children should become more comfortable saying short prayers together as a family.)*

YOU ARE A SPECIAL PART OF OUR FAMILY

Begin (or end) your family time by doing a fun family activity together, choosing an activity from your list of fun family time activities.

YOU WILL NEED:

- A soft ball (tennis ball or slightly larger)
- Several assorted household items placed inside of a large bag (such as a banana, a CD, a stuffed animal, a plastic toy, a granola bar)
- A Bible

ACTIVITY: CATCH THIS!

Begin by saying: **Let's do an experiment. I'd like to see who can stand up and catch this ball. I know that sounds easy, but there is one more thing. You can't use your hands or arms. I'll toss the ball, and let's take turns seeing if you can catch it.** Stand in front of your child and toss the ball gently in the air so that it lands right in front of her. Encourage creativity. Your child may try to catch it with her knees or even pin the ball on her chest with her chin. Let each child try a couple times, then move on.

ACTIVITY: MYSTERY OBJECT

Say: **Now, I want to see if you can tell what the mystery object is without using your hands or your eyes. So you can't touch the object or look at it. You can smell it if you want to. Everybody got it? Okay, who wants to go first?** Have one child close her eyes and put her hands behind her back. Choose one mystery object from the bag and hold it about four inches in front of her face, allowing her to smell the object. Then have her guess what the object is. After she has guessed, let her take a look at the object. Then let another child guess a different object.

ACTIVITY: HERE TO THERE

Place a marker, such as a sock, magazine, or small pillow on the floor about fifteen feet away from where you are with a clear path between you and the marker. For even better results, make sure that the path includes a turn, so that it is not a straight line. *Say:* **Now, I want to see who can get from here** *(where you are standing)* **to that marker without using your feet, your legs, and one of your arms. You can use any other body part you want.** *(Your kids may try to roll or pull themselves along the path with their arms. Make sure they stay on the path and do not use their legs and use only one arm. Even if they make it, it will take a lot of effort.)*

ACTIVITY: THE EASY WAY

Say: **For the final part of our experiment, let's see how easy it is when we use our body the way God wants us to.** Choose one child and have him catch the ball using his hands. Then have him identify a mystery object while looking at it. Finally, have him walk to the marker normally.

DISCUSSION: YOU ARE A SPECIAL PART OF OUR FAMILY

Have everyone sit down and read 1 Corinthians 12:14–26. *(If possible, have one of your children read it.)* Ask the following discussion questions:

1. **What does the Bible say about how Christians are like a body?** *(We are all different, we have important jobs, we are all valuable to God, we should look after each other.)*
2. **How hard was it to catch the ball, figure out the mystery object, or reach the marker when you couldn't use the right parts of your body?**
3. **What do our experiments show us about how important all the parts of our bodies are?** *(Every part of our body has an important job, it is much harder to do things when all of the parts are not working.)*

4. **How much easier was it to do the experiments when you could use all the parts of your body the right way?**
5. **How is our family like a body?** *(God made us, we are all different, we are all connected, we all help each other.)*
6. **What is one special way that each of us helps our family?**
7. **Just like God made all of the body parts to be connected together, what are some ways that we can stay connected, or close with each other?** *(Have family times, play games together, share, talk together, do things the other person likes, ask others how they are doing.)*
8. **Just like God made all of our different body parts to help each other, what are some ways that we can help each other as a family, so our family works just like God wants it to?** *(Be considerate, talk nicely, listen to parents, share, let someone else go first, encourage each other, say please and thank you, ask if someone needs help.)*

CLOSING PRAYER

Have each family member thank God for one thing that is special about the person on his right. Then, have a parent close in prayer, thanking God for the special characteristics that God has given to each member of your family. Ask God to help you all work at staying connected with each other so that you can have fun together and be the family God wants you to be.

GOD HAS BIG PLANS FOR YOU

Begin (or end) your family time by doing a fun family activity together, choosing an activity from your list of fun family time activities.

YOU WILL NEED:

- An apple and an orange
- A Bible
- Photographs of a cocoon, a butterfly, an acorn, an oak tree, a boy, and a girl (You'll find pictures of all these items on my website, www.parentlifesaver.com. Just go to the page corresponding to this book and look under the Family Time Discussion Guide section. Follow the directions on the page, print out the pictures, and have fun with your family time!)

ACTIVITY: COMPARING APPLES AND ORANGES

Say: **I'm going to make two statements. Listen carefully to each one.** *(Hold an apple in front of you.)* **Apples are good for you and oranges are bad for you.** *(Hold up an orange.)* **No, oranges are good for you and apples are bad for you.**

Discuss the following questions:

1. **Which statement is correct?**
2. **Are apples good for you? Are oranges good for you?**
3. **Are either apples or oranges bad for you?**

Hold the apple in one hand and the orange in the other. *Say:* **Here is another statement. Listen. Apples are good for you and oranges are good for you too. They are different but they are both good.**

Discuss the following questions:

1. **Who made apples and oranges?** *(God)*
2. **What do we have in common with apples and oranges?** *(God made us, we are different from each other, we all have good things about us.)*
3. **Should an apple feel bad if it is not like an orange, or should an orange feel bad if it is not like an apple?** *(No, God made apples to be apples and oranges to be oranges.)*

Read Psalm 139:13–16. Ask the following discussion questions:

1. **Who made each one of us?**
2. **Does God want (child #1) to be just like (child #2), or does God want (child #1) to be like (child #1)?** *(God wants child #1 to be everything he made child #1 to be.)*

Summarize: God made an apple different from an orange, and he made them both good, exactly like he wanted them to be. In the same way, he made each of us different from each other, and he wants each of us to be the special person that he made us to be.

ACTIVITY: WHAT'S ON THE INSIDE

Say: **Take a look at this picture.** *(Hold up picture of caterpillar.)* **How would you describe this picture? Now, after a caterpillar goes into its cocoon, what happens to it?** *(Hold up picture of butterfly.)* **Can you believe that this beautiful butterfly came from this tiny caterpillar?**

Say: **Take a look at this picture.** *(Hold up picture of an acorn.)* **How would you describe this picture? Now, when this acorn is planted into the ground, what happens to it?** *(Hold up a picture of an oak tree.)* **Can you believe that this huge, wonderful tree came from this tiny little seed?**

Read Jeremiah 29:11. Hold up the picture of a boy. *Ask:* **What is this picture of? What kind of plans do you think God might have for this boy?** *(to tell lots of people about Jesus, to be a football player, to help people who are poor, to be a policeman, to be a great daddy, etc.)* Hold up the picture of a girl. *Ask:* **What is this picture of? What kind of**

plans do you think God might have for her? *(to tell lots of people about Jesus, to be a teacher, to be a doctor, to help kids who are mixed up, to be a great mommy, etc.)*

Say: **Just like there is a beautiful butterfly hidden inside a tiny caterpillar and a huge tree hidden inside a tiny seed, God has wonderful plans for each of us that we may not be able to see right now. But they really are there. What are some of the plans that God may have for each of us?** Make a potential list of God's plans for each person in your family. Be creative!

ACTIVITY: THE REAL WINNER

Read this short story and then choose from the following discussion questions:

Devon was thirteen years old and was really good at basketball. Whenever he played basketball with his ten-year-old brother, Blake, Devon usually won because he was taller and had played longer.

Discussion questions:

1. **Does this mean that Devon will always be better than Blake at basketball? Why?**
2. **Do you think that Blake might be better than Devon at something else? Like what?**
3. **Say one thing that you're good at and one thing you're only medium-good at.**
4. **Do you think you can ever get better at your medium-good activity?**
5. **How important is _____** *(say each family member's name)* **to God?**
6. **How do we know that we're important to God?** *(Because the Bible tells us, because he died for us.)*
7. **If a boy or girl wasn't really good at very many things, would that boy or girl still be an important person to God? Would that person be important to his or her family?**
8. **Are we important because we are good at something, or because God made us?**

9. What is one thing that God has made special about _____
   _____ *(name each family member)?*

10. What is one way that we can each help make our family special?

SUMMARY

Say: Let's see if we can remember the three lessons we learned today. See if you can fill in the blanks. First, the apples and oranges taught us that even though we are all different, we are all made by _____ *(God)* and he wants us to be the special _____ *(person)* he made us to be.

Second, the pictures of the butterfly and the big tree taught us that it's what's on the inside that really counts, even if something looks really little at first. And inside of each of us, God has a special _____ *(plan)* that he made just for you.

In our last lesson, we learned that everyone is good at something. But what really makes someone important is not that they are good at reading or sports, but that they were made by _____ *(God)* and he loves them very, very much.

CLOSING PRAYER

Hold hands and have each family member pray for the person on his or her right. Have a parent say the closing prayer, thanking God for the different gifts he's given to each member of your family and asking him to help all of you learn to be encouraging with your words as you help each other become everything that God wants you to become.

THE FAMILY RESPECT RULE

Begin (or end) your family time by doing a fun family activity together, choosing an activity from your list of fun family time activities.

YOU WILL NEED:

- Several pieces of paper, scissors, and a pen
- A bag of M&Ms or other small treats
- A Bible

ACTIVITY: SHOWING RESPECT

Take a piece of paper, cut it to approximately the size of a dollar bill, and write "$1000" on it, decorating it as you wish to make it look like a $1000 bill. Show it to your children. *Say:* **This is a $1000 bill.** Then, with all the theatrical flair you can muster, begin to treat the $1000 dollar bill disrespectfully. Crumple it up. Throw it on the ground. Stomp on it. Eventually, rip it into pieces. Your children will be staring at you with wide-eyed disbelief.

Ask the following discussion questions:

1. **Was I treating the $1000 bill with respect?**
2. **Which is more important, a $1000 bill or our family?**
3. **If God wants us to treat our money with respect, how much more should we treat our family with respect?**

DISCUSSION: THE SIX STEPS FOR BECOMING A RESPECTFUL FAMILY

Step One: Discuss the importance of treating each other respectfully.

Read one or two of these passages: Colossians 3:12–21, 1 Corinthians 13:1–7, Galatians 5:22–25. Then discuss the following questions:

1. **What do you think *respect* means?** *(treating something with care, looking after it, treating it with honor, like you would treat something valuable)*
2. **Why do you think it's important for us to treat each other respectfully in our family?**
3. **What do you think God says about how we should treat each other?**
4. **How does it help our family if we treat each other like God wants us to?** *(Get along better, have more fun, stay closer to each other.)*

Say: **Let's make a list of words that describe what we want to be like as a family.** *(Take turns suggesting words and have a parent write them down.)*

Step Two: Introduce your children to the Family Respect Rule.

Say: **There's a rule that I think will really help our family. It's called the Family Respect Rule. It says that in a family, everybody needs to treat everybody else respectfully. All the time. Even if you feel mad, sad, tired, or anything. What do you think about that?**

Discuss the following questions:

1. **Would you like to be in a family where you are treated respectfully or disrespectfully?**
2. **If I get mad, is it okay for me to treat you disrespectfully just because I am mad, or do I need to be respectful even if I am mad?**
3. **How do you think the Family Respect Rule will help our family?**

Step Three: Define disrespectful behaviors (that you want less of) and respectful behaviors (that you want more of).

Say: **Let's make a list of disrespectful behaviors that we'd like to get rid of.** *(Take turns suggesting disrespectful behaviors, such as shouting, calling names, teasing, hitting, using other's things without permission, and so on. Have a parent write this list on a piece of paper.)*

Say: Now, let's make a list of respectful behaviors that we would like to do more of. *(Take turns suggesting respectful behaviors, such as sharing, using friendly words, taking turns, talking in a calm voice, and so on. Have a parent write this list on a piece of paper.)*

Step Four: Identify situations in which your children treat each other disrespectfully.

Say: Now, let's make a list of times when we treat each other disrespectfully, so that we can practice handling them differently. *(Make a list of situations that frequently end up in sibling conflict. Have a parent write this list on a piece of paper.)*

Step Five: Role-play those situations, having your children practice responding respectfully.

Say: Okay, let's choose one situation from our list and practice handling it respectfully. Which one should we work on? Choose one "problem" situation from your list and role-play it, having your children practice handling this situation in a respectful way. The parent can be involved in the role-play as well (if needed) and also acts as the director (saying, "Ready, set, action!"). You can also "freeze" the actors at any time, temporarily stopping the role-play in order to talk about what is happening at that moment. For example, if your children often argue about choosing a TV channel, set up a role-play where one child is watching TV and the other enters the room and wants to change the channel. Your goal is to help both children handle the situation with respectful words and actions (from your list of respectful behaviors). Make these role-plays short and fun, and toss your child an M&M or small treat when their role-play is through. Make sure to give your children plenty of positive feedback as they practice being respectful.

Step Six: Identify how handling the situation respectfully brought a positive outcome.

When you have completed the role-play, have everybody sit down and discuss the following questions:

1. **How would obeying God by treating each other respectfully, like you just did in that practice, help our family?** *(We didn't argue, didn't fight, didn't shout, we worked it out, no one got in trouble, we had more fun.)*
2. **What do you think would have happened if one or both of you would have handled that situation in a disrespectful way?** *(The person who was disrespectful would have immediately gotten in trouble, felt sad, lost privileges, disobeyed God, hurt our family.)*
3. **What do you think God thinks about the way we all handled things in these practices?**

CLOSING PRAYER

Have everyone identify one thing about themselves that the rest of the family can pray about. Give each family member a specific person to pray for. As you close your prayer time, ask God to help each of you work hard this week on following the Family Respect Rule by treating other family members respectfully. All the time.

SAY IT THE RIGHT WAY, RIGHT AWAY

Begin (or end) your family time by doing a fun family activity together, choosing an activity from your list of fun family time activities.

YOU WILL NEED:

- A $1 bill for each child
- A stinky sock (the stinkiest you can find!)
- A fresh, clean sock
- One sheet for each child with the two "When . . ." sentences written on them.
- A Bible

INTRODUCTION TO COMMUNICATION: DOLLAR BILLS AND STINKY SOCKS

Before you begin your family time, take the clean sock and place one $1 bill inside the sock for each child. So, if you have three children, place three $1 bills in the sock. *Then say,* **Today, we're going to work on how we talk to each other. Do we want to talk to each other in a way that hurts our family or helps our family?** *(Helps our family.)* **Right. The way we talk to each other is like these socks.** *(Hold up the stinky sock.)* **Look at this stinky, smelly sock. Does anyone want to take a smell? Would anyone want to stick their hand in this sock?** *(Probably not)* **If a burglar came in, would he look through the laundry basket to see if there was any money in this stinky sock? No, he wouldn't want to go near it. He'd run away gagging and choking.** *(Make a choking motion with your hands around your neck.)*

Continue: **It's the same way with how we talk to each other. You may have something very important and intelligent to say, but if you say it in a disrespectful way, it's like taking something valuable and putting it inside a stinky, smelly sock. Just like nobody wants to touch the stinky sock, will anybody want to hear what you have to say, if you say it in a disrespectful way?** *(No)* **That's right. So, we want to say things that are important and make sense, and say them in a respectful way. That would be like putting something valuable in a nice clean sock** *(hold up the clean sock).* **This sock is easy to touch. It even smells fresh and clean. Does anyone want to touch it? Now, if there was something valuable in this sock, we wouldn't mind putting our hand in and getting it, would we?** *(Reach your hand into the sock and give each child a dollar bill to keep, one by one.)* **In the same way, when you talk respectfully to another person, that makes it easy for them to listen to what you have to say. So we want to say things that make sense and say them in a respectful way.**

ACTIVITY: SAY IT THE RIGHT WAY

Say: **We want to talk respectfully to each other, even if we feel frustrated with the other person. One way to do that is to say what the other person is doing that you don't like and then say how you feel about it, or how it causes a problem for you. Here are two good sentences you can use.** Give each person who is old enough to read a sheet with these two sentences written on them, and then read them out loud.

"When you _____, *(name the problem behavior)*
    I feel _____." *(say how you feel)*
"When you _____, *(name the problem behavior)*
    then _____." *(say how it makes a problem for you)*

Say: **Let's do a few practices. See if you can use these sentences in these situations:**

1. **Naomi walks into Hailey's room and sits on her bed, wrinkling it up. How could Hailey use these sentences?**

(When you wrinkle up my bed, I feel kind of frustrated. When you wrinkle up my bed, then I have to remake it and I don't like that.)

2. **Isaac is doing his homework in his room and Amy turns on the television so loud that Isaac has trouble doing his homework.** *(When you turn the TV so loud, I get sort of frustrated because I can't concentrate. When you turn the TV so loud, it makes it hard for me to do my homework.)*

DISCUSSION: WHAT DO YOU THINK?

Ask: **Well, what does everybody think? Do you think these sentences would help us all talk more respectfully to each other? When are some times when we can use these sentences?**

Read Luke 6:31. *Ask:* **How does this verse relate to how we talk to each other?** *(God wants us to talk to each other the way we want the other person to talk to us.)* **What are the benefits of obeying God in the way we talk to each other?** *(We would get along better, we'd work things out faster, we wouldn't get into trouble, we'd have more fun.)*

ACTIVITY: PRACTICE SAYING IT THE RIGHT WAY

You can use situations that have caused sibling conflict in the past, or just make up a situation to practice. *Say:* **Okay, now let's practice using our sentences.** *(Here's a sample practice situation.)* **Let's say that Bryce is playing a computer game and his little sister, Nicole, is standing right behind him, giggling and going "Oooooh" and "Ahhhhh" as he plays. Now, Bryce is trying to do his best on this game, and his sister's comments are distracting him. Let's have someone be Bryce and someone be Nicole.** *(Choose actors for the role-play and have them take their positions at the pretend computer. Use a real computer if you have one nearby.)*

Continue, **Now, Bryce, show us what you could say to Nicole that would *not* be a good idea.** *("Get away from me," "Leave me alone!" "Go away, stupid!")* **Okay, Good job.**

What would happen to Bryce if he spoke so disrespectfully to his sister? *(He would go to time-out, have to stop playing the computer.)*

Now, how could Bryce use one of our two sentences so that he can respectfully tell Nicole what he thinks? *(When you stand* *behind me like that, I get a little annoyed because it's hard to play my game. When you make all that noise, I can't concentrate on my game.)* **Okay, now, Nicole, did that sound respectful to you?**

Now, let's try one more.

CLOSING PRAYER

Have each person say a short prayer, with a parent saying the final prayer. Ask each person to pray that God will help you to become a family that talks to each other in a respectful way. As you close, ask God to help each of you to remember the two sentences that you learned today and to use them when you feel frustrated with each other. In this way, you will be valuing each other as God's precious workmanship, and learning to obey him in all that you do.

TAKE TURNS TALKING

Begin (or end) your family time by doing a fun family activity together, choosing an activity from your list of fun family time activities.

YOU WILL NEED:

- One tennis ball
- A Bible

ACTIVITY: THE TENNIS BALL GAME

Have your children sit on the floor in a circle. *Say:* **Today we're going to work on how we talk and listen to each other. Here's how we're going to start.** *(Give one child the tennis ball.)* **Take this ball and toss it back and forth (or around the circle) ten times. Try not to drop it. Go ahead.**

When they have finished, say, **Let's think about what you just did. When you threw the ball to another person, what did you have to concentrate on?** *(Throwing it so that the person could catch it, not too hard or too soft.)* **After you threw the ball, what did you have to pay attention to?** *(Watching the ball so that you could catch it.)*

Say: **Playing catch with a tennis ball is a good example of what we have to do when we talk to each other. First, you have to say your ideas in a respectful way. That's like throwing the ball gently, making it easy for the other person to catch. Get it?**

Continue: **Then you have to pay attention and listen to what the other person is saying. That's like making sure you are watching the ball when someone throws it back to you. Do see how that works? So when we take turns talking and listening in a respectful way, it really helps us to work things out.**

ACTIVITY: THE TENNIS BALL DISCUSSION

Say: **Let's use the tennis ball to talk about some fun things we can do in our family times. Here are the rules.** *(Read and explain the Tennis Ball Discussion Rules.)*

1. **Only the person holding the tennis ball can talk.**
2. **If a person wants to say something, that person must raise his hand to let others know he has something to say.**
3. **Once the person with the ball has finished making his comment, he must gently toss the tennis ball to a person whose hand is raised.**

Toss the tennis ball to one of your children and begin your discussion. In addition to participating in the discussion, you also function as the referee and can guide the process along. Help your children to keep their comments short, and instruct them to toss the ball if they keep it too long. If you'd like, you can use a timer and have a thirty-second limit on how long any person can keep the ball before he must throw it. At various points during the discussion, choose a person without the ball to tell you what the person with the ball has just said. This sends the message that they all need to be listening intently to the person who is talking.

ACTIVITY: A REAL-LIFE TENNIS BALL DISCUSSION

Say: **You guys did a great job picking a family time activity and taking turns talking with the tennis ball. Now, let's try working through a real problem together, using the tennis ball to help us take turns talking.** *(Choose a relatively easy problem that your children recently experienced. If you can't think of one, make up a problem to practice on.)*
Say: **For example, let's say that you all want to play a game, but you all want to play a different game. Let's see how you would talk about it using the tennis ball to help you take turns talking and listening. Remember the rules—only the person with the ball can talk, and everyone else listens.** *(During the discussion, encourage your children to keep their comments brief and give random quizzes to see who is listening.)*

DISCUSSION: TAKE TURNS TALKING

Read Luke 6:31. *Ask:* **How does this verse apply to the way we listen to each other?** *(Listen to others if you want them to listen to you.)*

Read James 1:19–20. *Ask:* **What do these verses say about how God wants us to listen to each other?** *(He wants us to listen to others, not to get mad quickly.)*

Ask the following discussion questions:

1. **What lessons do we learn from the Tennis Ball Game that help us get better at talking and listening to each other?** *(It is more fun when everyone listens to each other, you don't have to shout, I like it when someone listens to me, we work things out better.)*

2. **Do you like it better when someone listens to you or when he or she ignores you?**

3. **When we take turns talking, does that help us work things out better or make it worse?**

4. **Do you think it would help to use the tennis ball sometime in a real situation to help us remember to take turns talking respectfully and listening to each other? Why or why not?**

CLOSING PRAYER

For your prayer time today, have everyone say a short prayer for all the other family members, asking God to help them in their daily duties (work, school, sports, activities). As you close in prayer, thank God for the privilege of being in a family that is working so hard on learning how to treat each other with respect.

SUGGEST A SOLUTION

Begin (or end) your family time by doing a fun family activity together, choosing an activity from your list of fun family time activities.

YOU WILL NEED:

- One or two cookies
- One or two dollar bills (and the equivalent in change)
- A Bible

ACTIVITY: THE COOKIE CAPER

Have one or two cookies to divide between all your kids (make sure that there are more kids than cookies). *Say:* **I have some really tasty cookies for you. But what I want you to do is to take turns shouting, "I want it!" back and forth ten times.** *(Yes, really)* **Go ahead.**

After they are done, ask: **How is the shouting working? Is it getting you a cookie?** *(No)*

Then ask: **Who can think of a good solution, or a good idea, to solve the problem of how you can all have some of the cookie?** Encourage your children to creatively think of a solution. One good solution is to divide the cookies by breaking them, or cutting them into small pieces. When they have thought of a positive solution, divide the cookie among them.

ACTIVITY: DO YOU HAVE ANY CHANGE?

Take a one dollar bill (or two dollar bills if you have three or more children) and hold it up in front of your children. *Say:* **I'd like to give this to you. But first I'd like you to take turns shouting, "I want it!" "No, I want it!" ten times each. Go ahead.**

Then ask: **How is the shouting going? Is it getting you anywhere?** *Ask:* **Who can think of a good solution, or a good idea to solve the problem of how to share this money with all of you?** Encourage your children to think of solutions. One idea is to change the dollar bills into coins and give each child the same amount in coins. When they have thought of a positive solution, divide the money among them.

DISCUSSION: SUGGEST A SOLUTION

Ask the following discussion questions:

1. **Did the shouting back and forth help you think of a good solution?** *(For younger children, you may have to explain what a solution is. A solution is the "best idea" for solving a problem.)*
2. **What does shouting usually accomplish?** *(Gets us into trouble, hurts our family, gives me a headache.)*
3. **How did it help when you suggested a solution?**
4. **Did your solution work out good for just one person, or for everybody?**

Read Luke 6:31 and 1 Corinthians 13:4–7. *Ask:* **What do these verses tell us about the kind of solutions God wants us to think of?** *(Solutions that we would like someone to do for us. Solutions that are kind and considerate. Solutions that work out well for everyone.)*

ACTIVITY: SUGGESTING A SOLUTION

Say: **Let's practice suggesting a solution, or a good idea, when we have a disagreement about something. What would be a good solution for these situations?** Read the following scenarios, helping your children to find a good solution to the problem.

1. **You each want to watch a different video for family movie night.** *(Just let the other person have her choice, let the other person watch hers this time and we'll watch mine next time, flip a coin, pick a number between one and ten, rock-paper-scissors.)*
2. **You each want to play on the computer at the same time.** *(Play the game together, let the other person go first, use a timer to each have the same time to play, decide who goes first by using rock-paper-scissors or a similar method.)*

3. **Everyone wants to go to a different restaurant for lunch.** *(Let parents decide, think of who hasn't chosen for a while and let him choose, just be happy to go anywhere, try to find a place everyone likes, find a place the most people like, take a vote.)*

DISCUSSION: HOW DID IT WORK?

Ask the following discussion questions:

1. **What did you like about the solutions you thought of?** *(They solved the problem, they were fair, no one got in trouble, we were respectful, it worked out the best for everyone.)*
2. **What would have happened if you had just argued or shouted at each other?** *(Sent to room, time-out, lose privileges, hurt our relationship.)*
3. **Which obeys God the most: finding a good solution or arguing with each other?**

CLOSING PRAYER

If you are married, have your children pray for each other (e.g., Drew prays for Ellie, Ellie prays for Taylor, etc.) and you and your spouse pray for each other. If you are a single parent, have your children pray for each other and you close with a general prayer for your family. Before you begin your prayer time, ask your children to each thank God (in their prayer) for one specific thing about the person they are praying for. As you pray, thank God for a family that is learning together how to obey him more and more each day. Ask God to help you all to learn to think of solutions that he would be proud of, solutions that are creative, considerate, and respectful to others. Close by thanking God for his forgiveness when we make mistakes and for his help in learning the lessons he wants us to learn.

WATCH OUT FOR HAZARDS

Begin (or end) your family time by doing a fun family activity together, choosing an activity from your list of fun family time activities.

YOU WILL NEED:

- Pictures of road signs (you'll find these pictures on my Web site www.parentlifesaver.com. Just go to the page corresponding to this book and look under the Family Time Discussion Guide section. Follow the directions on the page, print out the pictures, and have fun with your family time!)
- One sock for each person
- One package of M&Ms or similar small treats
- A Bible

ACTIVITY: ROAD SIGNS

Show your children the pictures of the various road signs. Discuss the following questions:

1. **What does this road sign mean?**
2. **What happens if a car doesn't pay attention to these road signs?** *(They may crash, get in an accident, people could get hurt or killed.)*

Say: **These signs tell us about danger or hazards. A hazard is something that could hurt you. Do we want to run into hazards, or do we want to stay away from them?**

ACTIVITY: HAZARD OR NOT A HAZARD

Say: **Now, just like there are hazards that you want to stay away from when you are driving, there are hazards that we want** to stay away from when we talk to each other. I'm going to say some words that describe different ways we can talk to each other. You tell me if it's a hazard or not a hazard. Read the following list, letting your children shout "Hazard" or "Not a hazard" following each item.

1. **Talking respectfully**
2. **Yelling** *(Hazard)*
3. **Saying please**
4. **Calling someone a name** *(Hazard)*
5. **Giving a compliment**
6. **Making a put-down** *(Hazard)*
7. **Saying, "Good job!"**
8. **Teasing someone** *(Hazard)*
9. **Making an encouraging comment**
10. **Saying something hurtful** *(Hazard)*
11. **Suggesting a solution**
12. **Using a disrespectful tone of voice** *(Hazard)*

Say: Let me read this list again. The good road signs include talking respectfully, saying please, giving a compliment, saying good job, making an encouraging comment, and suggesting a solution. The hazard signs include yelling, calling someone a name, making a put-down, teasing, saying something hurtful, and using a disrespectful tone of voice. Is that right?

ACTIVITY: SPOT THE HAZARD

Say: Here's what we're going to do. We're going to take turns acting out some scenes. If you are in the audience, your job is to watch for hazards. Anytime you hear someone saying a hazard, throw a sock at him.

Give each audience member a rolled-up sock and act out the following short role-plays. A parent should play one part and you can let each child have a turn as the coactor. In the role-plays, you are both acting as siblings. Make sure that you throw in some hazards, and be ready to get pelted with socks!

1. There is only one special snack left and two of you want it.
2. You are watching TV and your sibling comes in and changes the channel.
3. You both want to play a different game for family game night.

ACTIVITY: AVOID THE HAZARD

Say: Now, let's redo the role-plays, and this time whoever stays away from the hazards and says a good solution in a respectful way will get an M&M. If you are in the audience, then you are the judges and can say if we get an M&M. Replay each of the three role-plays, this time with no hazards. Suggest a good solution to the problem in a respectful way and enjoy your M&Ms.

DISCUSSION: WATCH OUT FOR HAZARDS!

Read Proverbs 12:18 and Psalm 19:14. Ask the following discussion questions:

1. **What do you think about hazards?** *(They are bad, I don't like them.)*
2. **What kind of words does God want us to use?** *(Words that are pleasing to him, words that help each other, encouraging words, respectful words.)*
3. **Why do we want to stay away from hazards?** *(They can hurt someone, they can hurt our family.)*
4. **How can we remember to use respectful words?** *(Remember that we don't want to hurt each other with our words, ask God to help us, just say how we are feeling, say how the person's behavior is a problem for us, suggest a solution, remember that whoever uses hazards will get in trouble.)*

CLOSING PRAYER

Have everyone say one thing that they are thankful for before you pray. Then gather any prayer requests. Have everyone pray for the person to the left, with a parent closing in prayer. Thank God for all the communication skills you have learned and practiced together and for how they are helping your family become closer. Ask God to help each of you continue to use these skills *(list them)* so that you can treat each other the way he wants you to.

LET'S SOLVE THIS PROBLEM

Begin (or end) your family time by doing a fun family activity together, choosing an activity from your list of fun family time activities.

YOU WILL NEED:

- A door with a key lock (like your front door)
- Several other keys
- The problem-solving steps and ground rules written on a piece of paper
- A plain piece of paper and a pencil or pen
- A Bible

ACTIVITY: FIND THE RIGHT KEY

Show your children a selection of five to ten different keys. Walk together to a door with a key lock (such as your front door). *Ask:* **Which of these keys do you think will unlock this lock?** *(The secret is that none of the keys fit the lock.)* Have your children take turns choosing one key and trying to fit it into the lock.

Ask: **How hard is it to open the lock when you don't have the right key?** *(You can't do it.)* *Say:* **Our problem is that we want to open the lock but we don't have the right key. Now, do you think this one might work?** *(Pull the right key out of your pocket.)* **Who wants to try?** *(Let each child have a chance trying the correct key.)*

Have everyone sit down in your family circle. *Ask:* **Which was easier, trying to open the door with the wrong key or with the right key? When we have a problem or are mad at each other, it is just like the door being locked. We need to find the right solution to solve the problem, just like the right key opens the door.**

DISCUSSION: GROUND RULES

Say: **We're going to learn five simple steps that will help us find the best solution when we have a problem or a disagreement. But first, there are certain rules that will help us to have a good discussion and think of the best solutions. Here they are.** Read the list of Ground Rules, explaining them as needed.

1. **No criticizing, name-calling, or put-downs.**
2. **Respect each other's views.**
3. **Take turns talking.**
4. **Be brief and to the point.**
5. **Three "zaps" and you're out for five minutes.**

Ask: **Does everyone understand the ground rules?**

ACTIVITY: PRACTICE SOLVING A PROBLEM

Choose a relatively simple problem that your children have recently had or one that they often encounter. Examples may include arguing over the TV, sharing the computer or video game system, sharing a certain toy, using each other's possessions, etc. Have a parent be the mediator (for giving zaps) and work through each of the problem-solving steps together. Remember to keep your discussion moving and comments brief and to the point.

Step One: State the problem. *Say:* **Now, let's try solving a problem together. In the first step, you say very clearly what you think the problem is in a respectful way. This helps us to find the solution faster. Okay, let's go around our circle and everyone can say how this situation is a problem for them in a respectful way.** *(Continue until this step is complete.)*

Step Two: Think of solutions. *Say:* **Okay, now we need to think of as many solutions as we can. Let's take turns suggesting possible solutions, or good ideas that might solve this problem. Who wants to go first?** *(Have each person suggest one idea at a time and continue until you have five to ten possible solutions. Write the solutions down on a piece of paper.)*

Step Three: Evaluate the solutions. *Say:* **Now we need to pick the best solutions. I'm going to read our solutions one at a time,** and if you think the solution would help, I want you to give it a plus. If you think it wouldn't help, then give it a minus. Okay, here we go. *(Read each solution and then give everyone a chance to rate it as a plus or minus. Record the ratings on your paper.)*

Step Four: Pick a solution. *Say:* **Let's see which solutions got the most pluses.** *(Read those solutions.)* *Ask:* **Now, which of these solutions on our plus list do you think will solve this problem the best?** *(Begin to devise a plan, using one or more solutions. Specify the details of how the plan would work.)*

Step Five: See if it worked. *Say:* **Now, let's try our solution, and in our next family time we'll talk about whether our solution worked or not. If it did, then great. If not, then we'll think of a better solution.**

DISCUSSION: SOLVING PROBLEMS THE RIGHT WAY

Read Ephesians 4:25–27, 29–32. *Ask:* **When we need to work out a problem, how do you think God wants us to do it?** *(Respectfully, telling the truth, controlling our anger, encouraging others, thinking about what is best for them, forgiving others.)*

Ask: **When we solve problems that way, how will that help us?** *(We'll have a better discussion, find a better solution, we'll obey God, we'll treat each other respectfully.)*

Summarize: **Anytime we need to, we can use our problem-solving steps to help us find a good solution to a problem. We can use them together as a family, or between any two people who are having a problem. You guys can use them anytime you need to. We'll practice them in another family time soon. And when we use our problem-solving steps in a respectful way, they'll always help us to find the best solution.**

CLOSING PRAYER

Go around in a circle, allowing each child to pray, with a parent closing in prayer. Thank God for his Word that gives us so much guidance for how to treat each other. And thank God for all the benefits of obeying him.

RESPONDING TO SIBLING AGGRAVATION

Begin (or end) your family time by doing a fun family activity together, choosing an activity from your list of fun family time activities.

YOU WILL NEED:

- Four sticky notes and a pen
- A Bible

ACTIVITY: LIKES AND DON'T LIKES

Say: **Let's start our family time by saying one thing that we like about each other. We'll take turns saying one thing we like about each person in the room.** Go around your family circle, with each person saying one thing they like about each family member. *Say:* **Now, when you live together as a family, sometimes all of us might do something that another person doesn't like. So, I'd like you guys** *(point to the children)* **to say one thing that one of your brothers or sisters does that you don't like too much. Remember, just one thing.** Have all the children identify one sibling behavior they don't like.

ACTIVITY: THE THINK/SAY/DO PLAN

Say: **When someone does something that you don't like, sometimes it's easy to do something disrespectful back to that person. Then what happens?** *(We both get in trouble.)* **That's right. So, I want to show you a plan that will help you handle it the right way when someone bothers you.**

Say: **I need a volunteer to show you the plan.** *(Have one child stand so everyone can see him/her.)* **You're going to be our model child.**

Your job is to stand right there and not move. Now, there are three parts to our plan, and we're going to put them on our model to help us learn them. Take one sticky note and write THINK on it. *Say:* **The first part of the plan is to think the right thing. What part of our bodies do we use to think with?** *(Our heads.)* **Right. So will someone stick this note to our model's forehead?** *(Have a child stick the sticky note to the model's forehead.)*

Say: **That looks great.** Write the word SAY on the second sticky note. **The second part of the plan is to say something that will help you handle the situation the right way. What part of our bodies do we use for that?** *(Our mouths.)* **Right, so will someone stick this to our model's mouth?** *(Have a child stick the note to the model's mouth.)*

Say: **Wonderful.** Write the word DO on each of the last two sticky notes. **The last part of the plan is to DO something. What part of our bodies should we use to show that?** *(Hands.)* **Will someone stick these two notes to our model's hands? Thank you.**

Ask: **What are the three parts of our plan?** *(Think, say, and do.)* **That's right. So we'll call it a Think/Say/Do plan.** *(Give the model a round of applause as he/she sits down.)*

DISCUSSION: THE THINK/SAY/DO PLAN

Say: **Let me explain each of the three steps. The first step is to think. We want to think something that will help us say and do the right thing, so that we handle the situation the right way— even if the other person doesn't. Remember, who is going to get into trouble, the person who is respectful or disrespectful?** *(Disrespectful)* **That's right. So, what do you want to be?** *(Respectful)*

Say: **So, if your brother or sister is doing something that bothers you, what is something smart that you can think, or say to yourself, that will help you do the right thing?** *(Help your children think of positive, solution-focused thoughts such as: Maybe he doesn't know this is bothering me; Just because she's going to get into trouble doesn't mean I have to; I'm going to handle this the right way; This is frustrating, but God will help me do the right thing.)*

Say: **Now, what would be something you could say to your brother or sister that would be smart and respectful and wouldn't**

get you into trouble? *(Help your children think of respectful things to say, such as: When you _____, then _____; Please stop _____; I asked you to please stop _____; If you don't stop, I'll get Mom.)*

Say: **The last part of the plan is to do something that will be respectful and solve the problem. After you have done the "think" and "say" parts of the plan, what is something that you can do so that you can solve the problem and not get yourself into trouble?** *(Help your children think of good solutions, such as: Ignore the person, go somewhere else, walk away and do something else, go and get help from your parents.)*

ACTIVITY: READY, SET, ROLE-PLAY!

Say: **Let's practice. Who wants to go first?** Decide on an "aggravating" situation and have the children role-play it, with one child bothering the other while the second child practices a think/say/do plan. Situations can include one child hitting the other, taking a sibling's belonging without asking, name-calling, making noise while the other person is doing homework or watching TV, etc. "Freeze" the action at certain points and have the second child tell you what he/she is thinking, and then show you what he/she would say and do to handle the situation respectfully.

Say: **That was great. You did a great job with your think/say/do plan. Who's next?** If time allows, give all children the chance to practice using a think/say/do plan in different situations.

DISCUSSION: HOW DID IT WORK?

Ask the following discussion questions:

1. **How do you think the think/say/do plan worked?**
2. **Why is the thinking part of the think/say/do plan so important?** *(It helps you stay calm, if you think the right thing then it's easier to say and do the right thing.)*
3. Read Proverbs 29:11. **When someone does something that bothers us, how does God want us to handle it?** *(Stay calm, be respectful, think of a good solution, walk away, ask them to stop.)*
4. **How does the think/say/do plan help you to obey God?** *(It helps us to think, say, and do the right thing.)*

5. **If you use your think/say/do plan in a respectful way, will you get in trouble, even if someone is bugging you?** *(No)*
6. **Who will get into trouble?** *(The person being disrespectful)*
7. **So, if one person is being disrespectful, the other person can still be respectful and think of a good solution. Is that right?**

CLOSING PRAYER

Ask each family member to pray for the person on the right, with a parent closing in prayer. Ask God to help your family to be more considerate of each other, so that you don't accidentally or purposely bother each other. As you pray, provide a humble model for your children by asking God to forgive you for any times that you have annoyed other people in your family, either accidentally or on purpose. Pray that God will help each of you to be thoughtful and considerate of each other, always treating the other person the way you would want to be treated. Thank him for his forgiveness and faithfulness and for always being with us.

SHARING

Begin (or end) your family time by doing a fun family activity together, choosing an activity from your list of fun family time activities.

YOU WILL NEED:

- A frequently used toy
- A Bible

ACTIVITY: I'M NOT SHARING WITH YOU!

Say: **Today, we're going to talk about sharing. Let's start by doing a role-play of not sharing. I need someone to act this out with me. We're going to pretend to be two kids playing and _____** *(your child's name)* **is going to ask me if he/she can use one of my toys. But, I'm *not* going to share. Then, we'll talk about it.** Using a toy or item that the children often play with, role-play two or three "sharing" situations where you have the toy and clearly refuse to share.

DISCUSSION: SHARING

Ask the following discussion questions:

1. **How did I do at sharing?**
2. **How do you think _____ felt when I didn't share?**
3. **If another person had seen me act that way, what would he have thought about me?** *(He's not very friendly, I don't want to play with him.)*
4. Read Luke 6:31. **What does this verse tell us about sharing?** *(If we want people to share with us, then we need to share with them.)*

5. Read Acts 2:44–47. **These verses tell us about the first people who were Christians. Does it sound like they shared with each other?**

6. **Why do you think God wants us to share with each other?** *(It is unselfish, it is friendly, it is a good way to show you love someone, it is a good way to make friends.)*

7. **What is one thing that you can share with someone else in our family?**

8. **What is something that you can share with your brothers or sisters?**

9. **Do you always have to share everything you have?** *(No)*

10. **What are some times when it is okay not to share?** *(If it is a special gift, if it is really breakable, if you are still using something, if someone doesn't take good care of your things.)*

DISCUSSION: MAKE A THINK/SAY/DO PLAN

Say: **Let's think of a think/say/do plan for sharing. Now, the first part is to think something that will help you say and do the right thing about sharing. What are some things that you could think when someone asks you to share?** *(Help your children think of positive sharing thoughts, such as: everyone has to share sometimes; God wants me to treat others the way I want them to treat me; if I share with _____, she'll probably share with me; sharing is a good way to have fun together.)*

Say: **Great. What is the second part of our plan?** *(Say)* **Right. So, what are some things you can say when someone asks you to share?** *(Help your children think of something friendly to say, such as: I'm using it now, but you can use it later; sure you can use it; maybe we can play with this together; maybe you can use this toy instead.)*

Say: **Okay. The third part of the plan is to do something. If you are going to share the toy with the person, then how should you give the toy to the person?** *(In a friendly way.)* **If you are still going to use it for a while, then how should you act to the other person?** *(Friendly)* **So, either way, how do you act to the other person?** *(Friendly)*

ACTIVITY: READY, SET, ROLE-PLAY!

Say: **Well, you guys are doing great! Let's give everyone a chance to practice. Okay, remember when I didn't share this toy earlier? Now, each of you will have a chance to show us how to share the right way.** Let each child role-play the situation you used in Activity #1. Freeze the role-play at certain times and have the sharing child say out loud what she is thinking and then show what she would say and do.

After the role-plays, say: **That was excellent. You all did a wonderful job. We'll practice again sometime.**

CLOSING PRAYER

Before you pray, go around your family circle and have everyone say one thing that he or she is thankful for. Have everyone hold hands as you pray. Ask the children to pray for the parents, and the parents will pray for the children. As you close in prayer, thank God for all that he has shared with us and given to us. Ask God to help everyone in your family to treat each other with the same love that he has shown to us.

TAKING TURNS

Begin (or end) your family time by doing a fun family activity together, choosing an activity from your list of fun family time activities.

YOU WILL NEED:

- An easy-to-set-up family game (such as a card game, dominoes, etc.)
- A Bible

ACTIVITY: I'M GOING FIRST!

Say: **Today, we're going to talk about taking turns. Let's all pretend that we are going to play** _____ *(say the name of the game)*, **but repeat what I say.** Have everyone sit as though you were going to play the game. Then say the following sentences in a humorous and overly dramatic way, having all family members repeat what you say, going one at a time around your family circle. When you have completed the first sentence, go on to the second, and so on.

1. **I want to go first.**
2. **No, I want to go first.**
3. **No, I said I want to go first.**
4. **If I can't go first, then I'm not going to play.**
5. **Fine, I didn't want to play with you anyway!**
6. **Well, fine then!**

Ask the following discussion questions:

1. **What kind of family do we sound like?**
2. **If we really acted like this, do you think any of our neighbors or friends would want to play a game with us?**
3. **If you heard a family talking like this to each other, would you want to play a game with them?**

DISCUSSION: TAKING TURNS

Read Philippians 2:3–4. *Ask:* **What do these verses tell us about taking turns?** *(God wants us to think of others instead of just ourselves, taking turns is one way of thinking of the other person.)*

Ask: **How is taking turns one way of obeying God?** *(We're treating others the way we want them to treat us, we're being considerate, it's friendly, it's not selfish.)*

Say: **Listen to this story: Justin and Ben are friends and they went outside to shoot some baskets. Ben ran under the basket and said, "Hey, Justin, pass!" Justin answered with a mean look. "No, I'm going first. It's my basketball."**

Ask the following questions:

1. **Did Ben act friendly?** *(Yes)*
2. **Did Justin act friendly?** *(No)*
3. **What was Ben thinking when Justin insisted on going first?** *(He must really want to go first, he's not being very friendly.)*
4. **If a group of kids were standing by the basket and heard the whole thing, what would they be thinking about Justin?** *(He's not very fun to play with, why is he acting that way?)*
5. **What could Justin have said or done that would have been much more friendly?** *(Passed Ben the ball, said, "Here you go," said, "Let's take turns shooting; you go first.")*

DISCUSSION: MAKE A THINK/SAY/DO PLAN

Say: **Let's make a think/say/do plan that will help us take turns the right way. What is something you can think that will help you to take turns?** *(Help your children think of positive thoughts for taking turns, such as: It doesn't just belong to me; Taking turns is considerate and that makes God happy; If I want to play I need to take turns; It's her turn now, and I'll go again when it's my turn.)*

Say: **Great. Now, what are some things you can say to show that you are going to take turns in a friendly way?** *(Help your children think of friendly things to say, such as: "Okay, it's your turn; you can go now.")*

Say: **Excellent. The last part of the plan is to do something with your body. What would you have to do to take turns?** *(Give the ball/dice/controls/game piece to the other person in a friendly way.)*

Say: **Who can say the whole plan: one thing you would think, say, and do to take turns in a friendly way?**

ACTIVITY: READY, SET, ROLE-PLAY!

Say: **Let's see how you can really do in practice. Let's pretend we are going to play our game again and this time you show me how well you can take turns.** Have everyone sit as though they were going to play the game from Activity #1. *Say:* **Who would like to show us how to take turns first?** When a child responds in a positive manner, such as, "Madeline, you can go first," give immediate praise for doing a good job.

Say: **Let's see how we can use our think/say/do plan for other situations. What is something you can think to help you take turns if your sister wants to join you in playing a computer game?** *(It's not just my game, we can both play and have fun, taking turns is one way of obeying God, if I want her to take turns with me then I should take turns with her.)* **What is something you could say?** *("Sure you can have a turn; as soon as my turn is over you can have a turn.")*

Ask: **What is something you can think if both you and your brother want to use the same toy?** *(I don't have to use it right now, I can use something else, it would be friendly to let him go first.)* **What is something you could say?** *(Explain why you need it, tell him he can use it, suggest that you take turns using it.)*

Say: **Let's see if you can fill in the blanks. When you give the person a toy, or the dice, or take turns or let another person go first, you should do it in a _____** *(friendly)* **way.**

Ask: **If you're having a hard time figuring out how to take turns and can't think of a good solution, you should get help from a _____** *(parent)*?

CLOSING PRAYER

Have each person choose another family that they know and pray for that family in their prayer time. As you close in prayer, thank God for helping your family to learn that a little thing like taking turns is one big way of obeying him. Ask God to help all of you think of each other before yourselves this week and to continue to shape you into the family he wants you to be.

BEING FLEXIBLE

Begin (or end) your family time by doing a fun family activity together, choosing an activity from your list of fun family time activities.

YOU WILL NEED:

- An object six to twelve inches long that cannot be bent (a strong branch, a wooden spoon, a metal rod)
- A large rubber band
- A Bible

ACTIVITY: BEND THIS!

Hold up the stick (or whatever object you are using) and pull on it to show that it will not bend. *Say:* **Sometimes, God wants us to be strong, like this stick that doesn't bend. What is one time when God wants us to be strong and unbendable?** *(When others are doing something wrong, to stand up for what is right, when we are tempted to sin.)*

Say: **What if the stick were here** *(firmly hold the stick upright in one hand)* **and needed to stretch or bend over here?** Point to a spot about eight to twelve inches to one side of the stick. **If I try to make the stick bend, what will happen to it?** *(It will break.)*

Say: **But what if I used a rubber band? If I hold the rubber band here,** *(hold the rubber band with two fingers)* **and someone holds it here,** *(have a child hold the other end of the rubber band),* **then it could still stretch over here, where the stick couldn't go.** Using your other hand, stretch the rubber band about eight to twelve inches to one side, forming a triangle.

Say: **Sometimes, God wants us to be strong, like the stick. But other times, God wants us to be flexible, like this rubber band.**

Flexible means that something can bend or stretch. When we are flexible with each other, it means that we can stretch and handle it when something doesn't go exactly our way. We stay respectful even if we can't do exactly what we want to do. **Can someone give me an example of a time when you should be flexible with our family?** *(When someone else is using something I want to use, when I don't get my way, when we go where someone else wants to go instead of where I want to go, when I have to wait my turn.)* *Say:* **That's right. So, God wants us to be strong at the right times and flexible at the right times.**

DISCUSSION: BEING FLEXIBLE

Read Ephesians 5:1 and Philippians 2:4. Ask the following discussion questions:

1. **When Jesus left heaven to come to earth and give his life for us, who was he thinking of, himself or us?** *(Us)*
2. **If we want to be imitators of God, should we only be thinking about what is best for us, or think about what is best for others too?** *(We should think about others too.)*
3. **When the Bible says that we should look not only to our own interests, but also to the interests of others, what does that mean?** *(We should think about what others want to do, do what is best for them, not always have to have our way.)*
4. **How does being flexible when we don't get our way, like this rubber band, help our family?** *(We help each other, we do what the other person wants to do, we get along better, there is less fighting, we have more fun, we don't always have to have our own way.)*
5. **What happens if you are not flexible?** *(You get mad, you get in trouble, you go to time-out, you still don't get your way.)*

DISCUSSION: MAKE A THINK/SAY/DO PLAN

Say: **Okay, let's make a think/say/do plan that will help us be flexible with each other, just like this rubber band. Remember, if we think the right thing, it will help us to say and do the right thing. What are some things that we can think that will help us be flexible if things aren't going exactly our way?** *(Help your chil-*

dren think of some flexible thoughts, such as: I can't always get my way, I can have fun doing what she wants this time, Maybe I can do it my way some other time, It would be friendly to let _____ do it her way this time.)

Say: **That was great. Now, what are some things that you can say to show that you want to be flexible, just like our friendly rubber band?** *(Help your children think of respectful things to say to show that they are flexible, such as: "We can do it your way this time; that's okay; I don't mind; maybe we can do what I want some other time.")*

Say: **Excellent. Now, what would you do to show with your actions that you are being flexible?** *(Wait your turn, talk respectfully, play what the other person wants, act friendly, find something else to do.)*

ACTIVITY: READY, SET, ROLE-PLAY!

Say: **Just for fun, let's see what would happen if someone was *not* flexible.** Choose a situation where your children have had difficulty being flexible with each other, such as choosing a movie or waiting to play a game. Place each actor in position and tell each actor her role, with one actor showing how not to be flexible.

Say: **Ready, set, action!** Freeze the role-play at the appropriate time to let the "inflexible" actor say what she is thinking that will help her do the WRONG thing. Then have her show what she would say or do that would NOT be flexible, such as shout, throw a fit, pout, etc.

Ask the following questions:

1. **How do you think that worked out?**
2. **What would happen to _____ if she really acted that way?** *(Get in a lot of trouble, go to time-out, hurt our family.)*

Say: **Now, let's try acting it out the right way to see if our think/say/do plan will work.** Have the actors replay the same situation, but this time, show how they would be flexible. Freeze the role-play at the right time to let the "flexible" actor say what she is thinking to help her be flexible. Then have her show what she would say and do.

Ask the following questions:

1. **Did _____ show us how to be flexible?**

2. **How do you think it worked out for everyone?**
3. **Even though _____ didn't get her way, did she do the best thing?**
4. **What do you think God thought about the way _____ handled it?**
5. **What do you think about being flexible?**

CLOSING PRAYER

After gathering prayer requests, hold hands in your family circle and ask each person to pray for the person on the left. As you close, ask God to help all of you to remember how much Jesus gave up for us when he came to earth. Pray that you will not just think of yourselves this week, but think of what is best for the other person too. Thank God for all of the lessons he is teaching your family as he is helping you to become more like him.

I FORGIVE YOU

Begin (or end) your family time by doing a fun family activity together, choosing an activity from your list of fun family time activities.

YOU WILL NEED:

- One frequently used toy, object, or CD
- A Bible

ACTIVITY: LISTEN AND THINK

Say: **Today we are going to talk about forgiving each other. Listen to this story:**

> **STORY #1: William got a brand new bike for his birthday. His sister, Madison, asked if she could try it out. While she was riding it, she hit a bump, fell over, and scratched the paint on the side of the bike. She told William what happened and said that she was very sorry. William grabbed the bike from her and said, "You're so clumsy, you can't even ride a bike without falling off. I'm never letting you use anything of mine again!"**

Ask the following discussion questions:

1. **When Madison scratched William's bike, was it on purpose or an accident?** *(An accident)*
2. **Did Madison apologize to William?** *(Yes)*
3. **Did William forgive Madison?** *(No)*
4. **What do you think about the way William acted?**
5. **What would you have done if you were William?**

STORY #2. Megan asked to wear Carla's sweater. Even though it was one of her favorites, Carla let Megan wear it. During dinner, Megan got ketchup on the sweater. When she told Carla about it and said she was sorry, Carla said, "Oh, no! Well, that's okay. I know accidents can happen to anyone."

Ask the following discussion questions:

1. **Did Megan get ketchup on Carla's sweater on purpose or by accident?** *(Accident)*
2. **Did Megan apologize?** *(Yes)*
3. **Did Carla forgive Megan?** *(Yes)*
4. **What do you think about the way Carla acted?**
5. **What would you have done if you were Carla?**

DISCUSSION: FORGIVING EACH OTHER

Read Colossians 3:12–14. Ask the following discussion questions:

1. **How does God want us to treat each other?** *(Be kind, gentle, patient, forgiving.)*
2. **What should we do if we act disrespectfully to another person?** *(Apologize, say we're sorry.)*
3. **What does God want us to do if someone does something that we don't like, but then apologizes?** *(Forgive them.)*

Read Isaiah 1:18 and Matthew 6:14–15. Ask the following discussion questions:

1. **What does God do when we ask him to forgive us?** *(Makes our sins as white as snow.)*
2. **If we want God to forgive us when we sin, what do we have to do when other people sin against us?** *(Forgive them.)*
3. **What are some things that we might need to forgive each other for in our family?** *(If we bother each other, shout, hit, say mean words, act disrespectfully, etc.)*

DISCUSSION: MAKE A THINK/SAY/DO PLAN

Say: **Let's make a think/say/do plan to help us when we need to forgive someone in our family. What are some things you can** think when someone says he's sorry for something? *(Help your children think of "forgiving" thoughts, such as: I do some things that I shouldn't do too; God wants me to forgive him; everyone makes mistakes; sometime I'll probably have to ask her to forgive me too.)*

Say: **Now, what is something you can say when someone asks you to forgive them?** *(Help your children think of things they can say to show that they accept the person's apology, such as: "That's okay; I didn't like that very much but I forgive you; we all make mistakes so I forgive you; forget about it.")*

Say: **Okay. Now, what can you do after you have forgiven the person to show him that you have really forgiven him?** *(Help your children think of friendly things to do, such as: pat him on the back, go on with normal activities, shake hands, hug.)*

ACTIVITY: READY, SET, ROLE-PLAY!

Say: **Let's practice. First, let's see what happens when a person does *not* forgive. We'll need two actors. Let's pretend that _____** *(first child)* **was using this item** *(hold up a toy or CD)* **that belongs to _____** *(second child)*. **Somehow, the item got broken and now _____** *(first child)* **is bringing it back to _____** *(second child)* **to tell him/her that it is broken.** Place the children in their positions.

Say: **Is everyone ready? Remember, I want _____** *(second child)* ***not* to forgive _____** *(first child)*. **Okay, ready, set, action!** Freeze the role-play at the appropriate time to allow the second child to say what he is thinking that is making it hard for him to forgive. Then have him show how he would act. Repeat the role-play, giving each child an opportunity to not forgive the other.

Say: **Now, let's try the same thing, but this time let's forgive each other the way God wants us to.** Repeat the role-plays, having the actors show how they would be forgiving. Freeze the role-play at the right time to let the second child show what she is thinking to help her forgive. Then have her show what she would say and do.

DISCUSSION: TO FORGIVE OR NOT TO FORGIVE

Ask the following discussion questions:

1. **Which did you like better, the forgiving role-play or the not forgiving role-play?**

2. Which role-play do you think God liked better?
3. How did it feel when the other person did not forgive you?
4. How did it feel when you were the unforgiving person?
5. How does forgiving each other help our family? *(Helps us get along better, not stay mad at each other, obeys God, we will all make mistakes and need to be forgiven.)*
6. What kind of family do you want to have, one where we forgive each other, or one where we stay mad at each other?
7. What do we each have to do to be a family where we forgive each other? *(Remember our think/say/do plans, apologize when we do something wrong, remember we all make mistakes, remember that God wants us to forgive each other.)*

CLOSING PRAYER

Remind everyone to thank God for all the times he has forgiven us for our sins. As you close in prayer, thank God for his faithfulness and forgiveness, even though none of us has done anything to deserve it. Ask God to help us imitate him by remembering to forgive each other the way he forgives us. Thank him for the wisdom in his Word, and for all of the great lessons he is teaching your family.

OUR FAMILY CHECKUP

Begin (or end) your family time by doing a fun family activity together, choosing an activity from your list of fun family time activities.

YOU WILL NEED:

- Several sheets of paper and a pencil
- A Bible

ACTIVITY: THE FAMILY THERMOMETER

Say: **Today we want to check in with everybody to see how our family is doing. Let's start by taking our family temperature. I want each of us to rate how we are doing on a one-to-five scale, where five is the best and one is the worst.** With pencil and paper, draw five vertical thermometer shapes, one on each piece of paper. Place the number five at the top of the thermometer, the number one at the bottom, and the numbers two, three, and four in their respective places in the middle.

Say: **Okay, I'll ask the question, and then you answer with a number from one to five that tells how you think our family is doing. Everyone got it?** Read the following questions, one at a time, and let every person give their one-to-five rating. Mark the ratings on the scale by placing the first letter of each person's name by the number they choose.

Family Thermometer Questions

How are we doing at:

1. **Treating each other respectfully**
2. **Getting along with each other**
3. **Having fun together**

4. Learning about God together
5. Growing closer as a family

DISCUSSION: THE FAMILY THERMOMETER RATINGS

Ask the following discussion questions:

1. What do you think about our ratings?
2. What area are we doing the best in as a family?
3. What area do we need the most work in as a family?
4. What is one thing that you like about our family?
5. What is one thing you would like to change about our family?

DISCUSSION: REVIEWING THE SCRIPTURE

Say: **Let's take a look at a couple of the Bible verses that we have read in some of our past family times.** Read a few of the following verses or passages: Galatians 5:22–23; Ephesians 4:25–27; Colossians 3:12–15; 1 Corinthians 12:14–26; 1 Corinthians 13:1–7; Galatians 5:22–25; Jeremiah 29:11; Luke 6:31; James 1:19–20; Philippians 2:3–4.

Ask the following discussion questions:

1. What do these verses tell us about how we should treat each other in our family?
2. How are we doing at following those verses together?
3. Where do we need to improve?

ACTIVITY: REFOCUSING ON OUR GOALS

Say: **Let's make a list of goals that we have for our family, so we know what we are working toward. I'll read this sentence and let's take turns filling in the blank. I'll write down the things we say.** Take turns filling in the blank for the following sentence and write the family goals on a sheet for future reference.

I'd like to have a family that _____

_____.

Say: **Now let's make a list of things that each of us can do to help our family reach these goals. I'll read the sentence and we'll**

take turns saying one thing that we can do. Take turns saying one thing that each of you can do to help your family reach its goals. Write this list on a piece of paper for future reference. Go around your family circle as often as needed.

One thing I can do to help my family reach its goals is _____.

ACTIVITY: FUTURE FAMILY TIME TOPICS

Say: **Let's make a list of topics we want to talk about in our next few family times. We can choose from any topic we've already discussed or we can pick any new topic we want. Topics can include anything that will help us reach our family goals, grow closer to God, be more respectful to each other, or help us handle difficult situations at home, at school, or with friends. Any ideas?** Make a master list of possible topics and then choose three topics that you would all like to work on during your next few family times.

CLOSING PRAYER

Have everyone hold hands and ask each child to pray for your family. As you close in prayer, thank God for all that he has done in your family and ask him to continue to shape and mold your family into the family that he wants you to be. Pray that God will help each person in your family to listen to him as he points out areas for growth. Commit your future family times to God and ask that he will guide each of you as you follow him with all your hearts.

PRACTICE MAKES PERFECT SAMPLE RESPONSES

STEP ONE: CREATE A STRONG FAMILY BOND

1. "Mom and I have been talking, and we've decided that, because you all are so important to us, we'd like to have a regular family time together. We'd like to make it really fun, so we'll need ideas from everyone for fun things that we can do. We also want to talk about important things together, so that we can stay close as a family and learn how to follow God better together. This Sunday afternoon, we'll have our first family time. Does anyone have a suggestion for something fun to do?"

2. Start small and *gradually* increase the frequency of touch and verbal affirmations. Make your physical touches brief, gentle, and unintrusive. Similarly, slowly build the frequency of your verbal expressions of affection, starting with bedtime and adding them gradually during the daytime hours.

STEP TWO: CONNECT WITH EACH CHILD

1. Alex is fourteen years old. He is soft-spoken, shy, very intelligent, enjoys time alone, and has a few close friends.

   - Strength: does well at school
   - Weakness: shy around new people
   - Difficult situation: birthday parties, holiday gatherings
   - How I can help: practice simple conversation skills (e.g., making a greeting, memorizing three "conversation-starter" questions) with Alex

2. Katie is ten years old. She is moody, struggles with writing, and is stubborn and easily frustrated.

229

- Strength: can stand up for herself
- Weakness: insensitive to other's feelings
- Difficult situation: when something does not go her way
- How I can help: teach Katie how to calm down (e.g., deep breaths) and think (e.g., what is the best solution?) when she feels frustrated

STEP THREE: ELIMINATE COMPARING, LABELING, AND COMPETITION

Comparing

Appropriate comment: "Jimmy, I'd like you to chew your food with your mouth closed."

Appropriate comment: "Megan, you can choose to say what you think respectfully, or you can choose a time-out. It's your choice."

Labeling

Appropriate comment: "Suzanne works really hard at school and does a great job."

Appropriate comment: "Tommy, I don't like it when you talk as if you know everything. I know you have some good ideas, and I'd love to hear them. But it is much more fun talking to you when you listen to what others have to say."

Competition

Redirecting comment: "Joshua, good grades are fine, but I'm much more interested in how you talk to your sister. I'd like you to say something encouraging to her about her grades, right now, please."

Redirecting comment: "Darcy, show me how you can be excited about winning and be a good sport at the same time."

STEP FOUR: REQUIRE SIBLING RESPECT

1. Dad: "Danny, did you spit at Peter? Okay, Danny you're going right to time-out. You can tell me what happened when your time-out is over. Peter, you come over here right now and tell me what was going on."

2. Mom: "Hey, Katherine, that's no way to ask Emily to leave your room. I'd like you to apologize to her right now. Now, let's figure out how you two can work things out more respectfully."

STEP FIVE: IMPROVE SIBLING COMMUNICATION

1. "When you interrupt me when I'm on the phone, it makes me really mad."

   "I get really angry when you keep saying that!"
2. Immediately go to the computer room and say, "Hey, guys, if there's a problem here I want you to use what we've learned in family time. Who would like to say what the problem is first?"

STEP SIX: STEP TOWARD SOLUTIONS

1. "Linda, that's a zap. Please make your comments respectfully."
2. Possible solutions:

   Steven shower at night.

   Jenny get up fifteen minutes earlier to shower.

   Both have individual place for toiletry items.

   Both clean up own mess and hang up own towels.

   Jenny out of the bathroom at 7:15 A.M.

   Disrespectful behavior (shouting, name-calling) equals thirty minutes early bed that night for the offending person.

   Parents will do bathroom check. The person who leaves the bathroom a major mess will have extra bathroom cleanup that day.

STEP SEVEN: TEACH SIBLING SURVIVAL SKILLS

1. Responding to sibling aggravation:

   Think: *If I handle this the right way, I won't get into trouble.*

   Say: "Hey, if you would _____, I'd appreciate it."

   Do: Go get a drink to give yourself time to cool down and think.
2. Sharing:

   Think: *I can always use this _____ some other time.*

   Say: "How about if we take turns?"

   Do: Decide together how to take turns.

3. Taking turns:

    Think: *If I let her go first, that would be very friendly.*
    Say: "Would you like to go first?"
    Do: Let the other person go first.

4. Being flexible:

    Think: *If we do* _____ *now, we can do* _____
    next time.
    Say: "Well, it's not my favorite, but I'll do it anyway."
    Do: Decide to give it a try.

5. Forgiving each other:

    Think: *At least he said he was sorry.*
    Say: "Forget about it."
    Do: Suggest a fun activity.

STEP EIGHT: REINFORCE POSITIVE SIBLING BEHAVIOR

Sample responses:

1. Gently squeeze each of them on the shoulder and with a big smile, say, "You guys are both doing a great job of talking politely and being really friendly to each other. That helps us to have such a fun time. I hope we can do this all the time!"

2. Tell your children that every time you hear one of them make an encouraging comment (e.g., "Good job," "Nice try," "You did really well at that") to the other, you will make a tally mark on a record sheet. If they reach five in one day, they will get a happy face on the calendar for that day. When they get three happy faces in a row, the family will go on a special outing, such as bowling or going to a matinee movie.

STEP NINE: USE SIBLING CONSEQUENCES THAT WORK

1. "Guys, you need to figure out how to share that cookie in a respectful way, or nobody is going to have it. What are your ideas?"

2. Respond immediately. Depending on how severe you determine the situation to be, either redirect the children to work things out more respectfully, or send the offending parties directly to time-out.

STEP TEN: PUT THEM ON THE SAME TEAM

Sample responses:

1. Disrespectful behaviors:

   Negative touch (hitting, kicking, pushing)
   Shouting
   Name-calling
   Put-downs

2. Respectful behaviors:

   Sharing
   Encouraging comments (e.g., "Good job," "Thanks," "Nice try")
   Respectful words and tone
   Getting help from parents if not sure how to handle it

NOTES

STEP ONE: Create a Strong Family Bond

1. TV-Turnoff Network, *Facts and Figures about Our TV Habit* (www.tvturnoff.org).

STEP TWO: Connect with Each Child

1. G. Brody, Z. Stoneman, and M. Burke, "Child Temperaments, Maternal Differential Behavior, and Sibling Relationships," *Developmental Psychology* 23 (1987): 354–62; G. Brody, Z. Stoneman, and J. McCoy, "Contributions of Family Relationships and Child Temperaments to Longitudinal Variations in Sibling Relationship Quality and Sibling Relationship Styles," *Journal of Family Psychology* 8 (1994): 274–86.

2. C. Stocker, "Siblings' Adjustment in Middle Childhood: Links with Mother-Child Relationships," *Journal of Applied Developmental Psychology* 14 (1993): 485–99; J. Dunn, C. Stocker, and R. Plomin, "Nonshared Experiences within the Family: Correlates of Behavioral Problems in Middle Childhood," *Development and Psychopathology* 2 (1990): 113–26.

3. A. Kowal and L. Kramer, "Children's Understanding of Parental Differential Treatment," *Child Development* 68, no. 1 (1977): 113–26.

STEP THREE: Eliminate Comparing, Labeling, and Competition

1. G. Brody, Z. Stoneman, and M. Burke, "Child Temperaments, Maternal Differential Behavior, and Sibling Relationships," *Developmental Psychology* 23 (1987): 354–62; G. Brody, Z. Stoneman, and J. McCoy, "Associations of Maternal and Paternal Direct and Differential Behavior with Sibling Relationships: Contemporaneous and Longitudinal Analyses," *Child Development* 63 (1992): 82–92; C. Stocker and S. McHale, "The

Nature and Family Correlates of Preadolescents' Perceptions of Their Sibling Relationships," *Journal of Social and Personal Relationships* 9 (1992): 179–95.

STEP SIX: Step toward Solutions

1. J. Dunn and P. Munn, "Sibling Quarrels and Maternal Intervention: Individual Differences in Understanding Aggression," *Journal of Child Psychology and Psychiatry* 27 (1986): 583–95.

2. J. Prochaska and J. Prochaska, "Children's Views of the Causes and 'Cures' of Sibling Rivalry," *Child Welfare* 64, no. 4 (1985): 427–33.

3. Ibid.

4. R. Felson, "Aggresssion and Violence Between Siblings," *Social Psychology Quarterly* 46 (1983): 271–85.

5. G. Brody, Z. Stoneman, J. McCoy, and R. Forehand, "Contemporaneous and Longitudinal Associations of Sibling Conflict with Family Relationship Assessments and Family Discussions about Sibling Problems," *Child Development* 63 (1992): 391–400.

6. G. Brody, Z. Stoneman, and K. Gauger, "Parent-Child Relationships, Family Problem-Solving Behavior, and Sibling Relationship Quality: The Moderating Role of Sibling Temperaments," *Child Development* 67 (1996): 1289–1300.

7. C. Rinaldi and N. Howe, "Siblings' Reports of Conflict and the Quality of Their Relationships," *Merrill-Palmer Quarterly* 44, no. 3 (1998): 404–22.

STEP SEVEN: Teach Sibling Survival Skills

1. J. Dunn and P. Munn, "Siblings and the Development of Prosocial Behavior," *International Journal of Behavioral Development* 9 (1986): 265–84.

STEP EIGHT: Reinforce Positive Sibling Behavior

1. J. Prochaska and J. Prochaska, "Children's Views of the Causes and 'Cures' of Sibling Rivalry," *Child Welfare* 64 no. 4 (1985): 427–33.

2. H. Leitenberg, J. Burchard, S. Burchard, E. Fuller, and T. Lysaght, "Using Positive Reinforcement to Suppress Behavior: Some Experimental Comparisons with Sibling Conflict," *Behavior Therapy* 8 (1977): 168–82.

STEP NINE: Use Sibling Consequences That Work

1. J. C. Bennett, "Nonintervention into Siblings Fighting as a Catalyst for Learned Helplessness," *Psychological Reports* 66 (1990): 139–45.

2. M. Perlman and H. Ross, "The Benefits of Parent Intervention in Children's Disputes: An Examination of Concurrent Changes in Children's Fighting Styles," *Child Development* 64 (1997): 690–700.

3. G. Brody and Z. Stoneman, "Sibling Conflict: Contributions of the Sibling Themselves, the Parent-Sibling Relationships, and the Broader Family System," *Journal of Children in Contemporary Society* 19 (1987): 39–53; T. S. Allison and S. L. Allison, "Time Out from Reinforcement: Effect on Sibling Aggression," *The Psychological Record* 21 (1971): 81–86.

4. R. Olson and M. Roberts, "Alternative Treatments for Sibling Aggression," *Behavior Therapy* 18 (1987): 243–50.

You can contact Dr. Cartmell at
1761 S. Naperville Road
Suite 200
Wheaton, IL 60187
(630) 260-0606

For helpful parenting tips, articles, Q&A, and
more, visit Dr. Cartmell's website at:
www. parentlifesaver.com

We want to hear from you. Please send your comments about this book
to us in care of the address below. Thank you.

GRAND RAPIDS, MICHIGAN 49530 USA

WWW.ZONDERVAN.COM